# Hearts Unto Wisdom

The Curious Woman's Guide to
Understanding (*and Appreciating!*)
the Minor Prophets
of the Bible

## Gleniece Lytle

*Desert Rain Editions*

*Hearts Unto Wisdom: The Curious Woman's Guide to Understanding (and Appreciating!) the Minor Prophets of the Bible*
Copyright © 2025 by Gleniece Lytle

ISBN: 9798991068116
ISBN: 9798991068109 (ebook)

Published by Desert Rain Editions, LLC
PO Box 8163
Hualapai, AZ 86412

https://desertraingleniece.com
https://desertrainediting.com

Unless otherwise marked, all Scripture is taken from the Holy Bible King James Version (KJV).
Scripture marked (NKJV) is taken from the New King James Version®. Copyright © 1982 by Thomas Nelson. Used by permission. All rights reserved.

All Bible word definitions are taken from *Strong's Exhaustive Concordance of the Bible: Updated Addition*, Massachusetts, Hendrickson Publishers, 2007.

Bold italic and bracketed explanatory words within Bible verses were used for emphasis and clarity throughout this book.

Thank you, Janet Nash and Kathy Walter, for your helpful and much appreciated feedback.

Heart locket icon, *myvalentineslove*, courtesy of fontcafe.com
Dragonfly icon courtesy of Cah Nggunung via flaticon.com

*To my fellow curious Christian women*

# Contents

# Author's Note

This study is not a comprehensive, word-by-word, line-by-line exposition on the Minor Prophets. If it were, it would be a hefty tome. I subjectively chose what to include and what to leave out. Throughout this book, I leaned heavily upon Bible verse citation. I wanted you to know where I got the source for the thought or conclusion in each paragraph. The Word of God is the star, not me.

Within the Christian church, there are many eschatological positions regarding the great tribulation, the second coming of Christ, and the millennium, events spoken of throughout the Minor Prophets. I am not bound by any religious organization's persuasion or creed, and years of Bible reading has led me to disagree with amillennialism, post-millennialism, and several key components of dispensational and historic premillennialism because their assertions are not biblically supported (see the appendix for a short definition of each term). I also oppose the church's twentieth-century invention of the rapture for the same reason.

While these differing viewpoints within the church and between individual believers are not salvation-breaking issues worth arguing over (we will find out who's right soon enough), they do affect how each Christian lives their lives. As a curious Christian woman, I take the Bible at face value and let it interpret itself.

# Introduction

I have always been a curious woman. Curious about how the magnetic field works, why the prism splits the color spectrum, and how plants and animals build symbiotic relationships. Why do black holes exist and is there an end to space? How did we go from 1960s room-size computers to the ones we hold in our hands? Curiosity has pushed me to ask what it is, how does it work, what does it mean, why it is the way that it is, and how did it come to be. In grade school, I read every library resource I could find on the Loch Ness Monster, Bigfoot, and the Bermuda Triangle totally bummed to find out there wasn't a concrete answer. Sometimes, the answers are hidden, forever to remain a mystery until Christ returns. Certain cultural, historical, or end-times passages found in the Bible are no different. By its very nature, end-times prophecy invites curiosity. Like an intricate knotted puzzle, an enigma to be solved, we work to tease the threads apart. But it's only by God's Spirit that we're given wisdom to understand.

Welcome to my in-depth look into the twelve books commonly referred to as the Minor Prophets. These Old Testament books, starting with Hosea and ending with Malachi, are minor only in regard to their length—their "Minor" tag having nothing to do with their significance. I could argue that Hosea and Zechariah, at fourteen chapters, aren't minor at all. If length were the criteria, why wasn't the book of Daniel, at twelve chapters, included with the Minor Prophets? (Hmm. There's my curiosity at work again.)

To start off this study, it's a good idea to understand that in ancient Hebrew times, the Old Testament was divided into three part: (1) the **Law**, also known as the Pentateuch or Torah written by Moses: Genesis, Exodus, Leviticus, Numbers, and Deuteronomy, (2) the **Prophets**, beginning with the former: Joshua, Judges, Ruth, Samuel, Kings, Chronicles and ending with the latter: Jeremiah with Lamentations, Ezekiel, Isaiah, Daniel, and the twelve Minor Prophets, and (3) the Hagiographa, known simply as **Writings** which consisted of the books of Ezra and Nehemiah, Esther, Job, Psalms, Proverbs, Ecclesiastes, and Song of Solomon.

Later the Scriptures were divided into four parts: (1) the **Law** (same as above), (2) the **Historical** books consisting of Joshua, Judges, Ruth, First and Second Samuel, First and Second Kings, First and Second Chronicles, Ezra, Nehemiah, and Esther, (3) the **Poetic/Wisdom** writings consisting of Job, Psalms, Proverbs, Ecclesiastes, and Song of Solomon, and (4) the **Prophetic** books, subdivided into the Major Prophets: Isaiah, Jeremiah with Lamentations, Ezekiel, and Daniel, and the Minor Prophets: Hosea, Joel, Amos, Obadiah, Jonah, Micah, Nahum, Habakkuk, Zephaniah, Haggai, Zechariah, and Malachi.

There is much we women of God can learn from the books of the Minor Prophets. God's love, mercy, and righteous judgment shown to Israel and the nations round about them remain the same for us—God does not change. The prophecies meant for Israel and the surrounding nations all happened precisely as God said they would, so we can be assured the future ones will too—God does not lie. And lastly, the fears, stubbornness, and selfish pursuits of the Israelites are no different than our own—human nature is the same. But we have access to God's Spirit which makes all the difference in conquering what comes naturally to all of us.

I am not a Bible scholar. I'm merely a curious woman with questions, eager to know the answers and share what I discover with you. One of my most favorite sayings is "You learn something new every day." As we Christian women apply our hearts unto wisdom and tap into our God-given curiosity, no matter what we study in the Bible, it can lead to awe-inspiring, life-changing counsel. I hope you learn something new and wonderful in these chapters covering the Minor Prophets of the Bible.

*So teach us to number our days, that we may apply our hearts unto wisdom. (Psalm 90:12)*

# Hosea

*I will betroth thee unto Me for ever*

The book of Hosea is a poetic pleading from the Most High God to His wife, the nation of Israel. She had turned aside and taken other lovers without shame. Although God's fury and His pronouncements for Israel's destruction were justified, He made way for her to return, an undeserved forgiveness, if only she would. But He needed her to listen and see her treachery for what it was.

Enter the prophet, Hosea. This man glimpsed the pain God felt regarding Israel's adulterous heart when God commanded him to take a local whore to be his wife. Her name was Gomer. She wasn't a reformed prostitute; she wasn't like Rahab who repented of her past and was honored to be named among the lineage of Christ, her savior. No, this Gomer was an adulteress whom God told Hosea to love even though she couldn't be trusted, to love even though she wouldn't love him back like a faithful wife should (Hosea 3:1).

Marital fidelity is *the* foundation of a loving, thriving marriage. As a wife, being true to your spouse is one of the main cornerstones of righteous living. But if spouses stray, if a husband or wife turns away and embraces another, the emotional turmoil is tremendous. Wild anger, gripping sadness, and a desire for justice consumes the soul. We would never purposefully marry someone we knew from the start would fail us in this way, but the hand-picked servants of God were often told to do unusual things, things that went against common sense and their own feelings, in order to get the attention of the errant people of God they were instructed to warn.

Hosea's obedience to this odd request was necessary to rouse the unfaithful Israelites. They needed to see their own infidelity toward God and to think about their own duplicitous behavior and repent from it in order to stave off their imminent doom. God told the men of Israel He would refuse to punish their daughters for harlotry and their wives for adultery because they were all guilty of the same hypocrisy (Hosea 4:14). They would not get justice because their hearts were divided; they were not faithful to God nor to each other (Hosea 10:2). God provided for, protected, and cherished the nation of Israel as a husband ought to for his wife, yet the Israelites regarded their vow lightly as a duty to perform grudgingly instead of as a privilege to be loved by and to serve the living God.

In Hosea 7:13–15, God says to ancient Israel, "Woe unto them, they have fled from me . . . they have spoken lies to me . . . they rebel against me . . . they return, but not to the most High: they are a deceitful bow." Ancient Israel, as recorded throughout the Bible, often mirrors our own feeble attempts to live Christ-like without yielding fully to Christ. How so?

- Whenever we water down His Word to suit ourselves
- Whenever we worry that God cannot save us
- Whenever we believe that something else will fulfill us more
- Whenever we run to the world first for the answers to our problems

These inconsistencies in trusting God's hand in our lives—our lack of complete fidelity toward Him—reflect the same sinfulness in our modern times that Israel did in theirs.

## What's in a name?

Names and their meanings meant a great deal to the Israelite culture. God commanded Gomer's first child with Hosea to be called *Jezreel* which means "God will sow."[1] Jezreel was a city in ancient Israel remembered for its day of bloodshed, a reminder of the consequences of sin, where all the heirs of evil king Ahab and all the false priests of Israel who worshipped Baal were executed (2 Kings 10). God commanded Gomer's second child to be named *Lo-ruhamah*,[2] meaning "not having obtained mercy," and her third child, *Lo-ammi*,[3] meaning "not my people" (Hosea 1:6–9). These unlovely names reflected Israel's current status with God. Israel was under the delusion that it was both Ruhamah and Ammi—mercifully loved people of God—and that it could reap the benefits of that status without being faithful in return.

*All their wickedness is in Gilgal: for there I hated them:*
*for the wickedness of their doings I will drive them out of*
*mine house, I will love them no more: all their princes are*
*revolters. (Hosea 9:15)*

God hated Gilgal. But why exactly? Gilgal, which means *wheel* or *rolling* in Hebrew,[4] was the base camp where Joshua and his men conquered Jericho in the Holy Land seven hundred years earlier. God said to Joshua, "This day have I rolled away the reproach of Egypt from off you" (Joshua 5:9). Twelve stones, one for each tribe of Israel, were taken from the middle of the dried-up Jordan river (a lesser Red Sea moment, but just as significant), and with these stones, Joshua built a "gilgal," a circular monument, or memorial, for their miraculous passage through the Jordan river before the seven-day siege of Jericho started, and where Joshua later dedicated the victory of the defeat of Jericho to God. This is the same Jordan river where John the Baptist began his ministry and where Christ was baptized and the Holy Spirit descended upon Him. The original circular twelve-stone memorial represented the power of God in the lives of His children and a reminder for them to fear Him. From that memorial came the city of Gilgal, which was a place of worship and dedication to God. But in Hosea's day, it had become a place they'd forgotten their God, a city that worked iniquity and was polluted with blood (Hosea 6:8). A place known for its idolatry.

## Ephraim and the backsliding heifer

God led the Israelites out of Egypt with gentleness, lifted off their chains of bondage, and fed and cherished them. But in return, they behaved like a backsliding heifer (Hosea 4:16). God equated Israel to a stubborn, untamed cow trampling over His goodness and breaking the enclosures He provided for her safety. She did not submit to the yoke of the law of God, and in rebellion turned away, sliding back through the muck and mire to the abominable ways of the past. All of us have behaved this way at some point in our lives. But with God, there is always hope. He does not leave us in the muck of our sins if we repent.

> *I will not execute the fierceness of mine anger, I will not return to destroy Ephraim: for I am God, and not man. (Hosea 11:9)*

> *I will heal their backsliding, I will love them freely: for mine anger is turned away from him. (Hosea 14:4)*

Ephraim is mentioned repeatedly in the book of Hosea alongside Israel and Judah. Ephraim was the second son of Joseph by his Egyptian wife, Aseneth, when he was promoted to second-in-command by Pharaoh in Egypt. The name *Ephraim* in Hebrew means "double fruit."[5] Later in Israel's history, the tribes split into two kingdoms: the northern (Israel) and southern (Judah) kingdoms. Ephraim became the largest tribe in Israel, and in biblical writings like the book of Hosea, the word *Ephraim* is sometimes substituted for *Israel* as a whole.[6]

"Ephraim is oppressed and broken in judgment, / Because he willingly walked by human precept" (Hosea 5:11 NKJV). The people of God ran after the abominable ways of the nations around them instead of staying true to the covenant of God. The more they gained physically, the more they transgressed spiritually, plowing wickedness, reaping iniquity, and eating the fruit of lies. (Hosea 4:7; 10:1, 13; 13:6). Yet, despite how much wealth she had, Israel was an empty vine that brought forth fruit unto herself and denied the truth God spoke in Hosea 14:8, "From me is thy fruit found." Sadly, many Christians today allow their blessings (time, money, possessions) to become barriers to their spiritual growth, oblivious to being led by the spirit of whoredoms (Hosea 5:4). As the faithful bride of Christ, as humble women of God, do we acknowledge where our fruit is found and glorify God because of it?

> For she did not know that I gave her corn, and wine, and oil, and multiplied her silver and gold, which they prepared for Baal. (Hosea 2:8)

> He that abideth in me, and I in him, the same bringeth forth much fruit: for without me ye can do nothing. (John 15:5)

The book of Hosea reveals how Israel viewed her great blessings, not as coming directly from the hand of God, but as gifts of service given to her by her lovers. These lovers were other cultures and kingdoms and pagan ideologies that wooed Israel away. She hadn't passively allow herself to be pursued either. This was no coquettish blush behind a veil. She eagerly ran after her lovers and felt no shame in her adultery. But for all this, God said He would "speak comfortably unto her" after her harlotry to woo her back to Himself, even though He had every right to cast her aside for good (Hosea 2:14). This is the goodness and mercy of God and points to the glorious hope we have in Christ. Because with God there is always hope for those who repent.

The Bible most often uses the phrases "in that day," "at that day," "in the latter days," and especially, "the day of the Lord" to refer to Jesus Christ's second coming, but sometimes "at that day" refers to when He would enter the world the first time to provide forgiveness of sins and salvation through faith in His name. "And it shall be at that day, saith the Lord, that thou shalt call me Ishi [husband]: and shalt call me no more Baali [Master]" (Hosea 2:16). In the Old Testament, the law of Moses was Israel's master, but even back then God said, "For I desired mercy, and not sacrifice; and the knowledge of God more than burnt offerings" (Hosea 6:6).

In the New Testament, Christ was born to take on the role of husband and to fulfill the law eradicating the need for a master. But Israel's leaders, who read the law daily, refused to acknowledge the Messiah it spoke about throughout its parchment pages. They preferred bondage to the law over freedom in Christ. They preferred to control their "master," than to release their hold in faith. Jesus Christ spoke to the self-righteous Pharisees in Matthew quoting Hosea, "But go ye and learn what that meaneth, I will have mercy, and not sacrifice: for I am not come to call the righteous, but sinners to repentance (Matthew 9:13). The Pharisees thought they were already righteous—a dangerous place for anyone to be in—when in reality, they were destroying themselves for lack of knowledge of their need for a savior (Hosea 4:6).

Like most Old Testament books, the book of Hosea is filled with parallels of the prophecy of the coming Messiah and the redemption of spiritual Israel.

| | |
|---|---|
| *Yet the number of the children of Israel shall be as the sand of the sea, which cannot be measured nor numbered. (Hosea 1:10)* | Spiritual Israel cannot be numbered, like the sand of the sea, because all faithful people become the children of God no matter their cultural lineage.[7] |
| *So I bought her to me for fifteen pieces of silver, and for an homer of barley, and an half homer of barley. (Hosea 3:2)* | Hosea bought Gomer just as Christ bought and paid for us, His bride, through His sacrificial blood. |
| *Afterward shall the children of Israel return, and seek the Lord their God, and David their king; and shall fear the Lord and his goodness in the latter days. (Hosea 3:5)* | To "seek . . . David their king" is a reference to Jesus Christ, who came from the lineage of David and is our King of Kings and Lord of Lords. |

| | |
|---|---|
| *Come, and let us return unto the Lord: for he hath torn, and he will heal us; he hath smitten, and he will bind us up. After two days will he revive us: in the third day he will raise us up, and we shall live in his sight.* *(Hosea 6:1–2)* | When we return to God, He will bind up our wounds and heal us. And on the "third day" (a reference to Christ's own resurrection), He will raise us up, and we will forever live with Him. |
| *And by a prophet the Lord brought Israel out of Egypt, and by a prophet was he preserved.* *(Hosea 12:13)* | There is a wealth of duality in this verse. By a prophet (Moses/physical, Christ/spiritual), the Lord brought Israel (physical nation/spiritual children) out of Egypt (physical place of bondage/spiritual bondage) and by a prophet was he preserved (Moses led the Israelites to physical safety/Christ leads us to spiritual safety). |

Twice the apostle Paul used scriptural references from the book of Hosea. In Romans chapter 9, he took Hosea 1:10 and 2:23 respectively in an almost identical rendering and made the correlation between who we used to be and who were are now in Christ Jesus.

> *As he saith also in Osee* [Greek spelling of Hosea], *I will*
> *call them my people, which were not my people; and*
> *her beloved, which was not beloved.*
> *And it shall come to pass, that in the place where it was*
> *said unto them, Ye are not my people; there shall they*
> *be called the children of the living God.*
> *(Romans 9:25–26)*

Paul, quoting Hosea 13:14, looked forward to the day when sin and death would be destroyed. "O death, where is thy sting? O grave, where is thy victory? The sting of death is sin; and the strength of sin is the law" (1 Corinthians 15:55). Paul knew death's sting came from our sinful human nature and sin's strength came from our inability to live perfectly by the righteous law of God. But thanks be to God who gave us the victory over death through our Lord Jesus Christ.

> *I will ransom them from the power of the grave; I will*
> *redeem them from death: O death, I will be thy plagues;*
> *O grave, I will be thy destruction: repentance shall be hid*
> *from mine eyes. (Hosea 13:14)*

## The goodness and severity of God

In Hosea 2:15, God told Israel He would trade "the valley of Achor for a door of hope." What is the significance of the valley of Achor? In Joshua 7:26, after the famed battle of Jericho, one of the men of Israel did exactly what God said not to do. He stole gold and silver and accursed idols from that city and hid them in his tent. Did he think he could fool God? Not only did he condemn himself, but all his family were dragged out to the valley of Achor and stoned with him. Everything he had was destroyed. The valley of Achor was synonymous with judgment and death. The penalty for adultery was the same. But God loves us dearly and provides us an escape from our sentence of death— His Son whom we are betrothed to now. He is our door of hope.

> *And I will betroth thee unto me for ever; yea, I will betroth thee unto me in righteousness, and in judgment, and in lovingkindness, and in mercies.*
> *I will even betroth thee unto me in faithfulness: and thou shalt know the Lord. (Hosea 2:19–20)*

There is no greater purpose in life than to know the Lord (John 17:3). But Israel didn't want to know. They chose to cast off that which was good—the knowledge of God—and went about to establish their own truth, only to become prey to their enemies (Hosea 8:3). When we embrace anything God calls an abomination, we, like the Israelites, lie in bed with the enemy of our souls.

> *My people are destroyed for lack of knowledge: because thou hast rejected knowledge, I will also reject thee, that thou shalt be no priest to me: seeing thou hast forgotten the law of thy God, I will also forget thy children. (Hosea 4:6)*

> *They will not frame their doings to turn unto their God: for the spirit of whoredoms is in the midst of them, and they have not known the Lord. (Hosea 5:4)*

*I have written to him the great things of my law, but they were counted as a strange thing. (Hosea 8:12)*

We are all adulteresses by nature. Sobering thought, but true. And that's what the story of Hosea is all about. It's about us

- casting aside our God, our husband, for another;
- going after the world for wisdom;
- letting strangers (worldly ideologies, monetary possessions, social distractions, etc.) take our strength and trading it for trinkets;
- burning up our judges (tolerating sin in ourselves and others) and wondering why we're in trouble (Hosea 7:7–9).

Faith in Christ changes an adulteress into a chaste bride of Christ. But like the unwise virgins who thought they knew the Bridegroom, we need to resist complacency and be diligent to know our God. Hosea 8:2 says, "Israel shall cry unto me, My God, we know thee." This will also be the cry in the end times from those who say they believe. But Christ's response will be, "Verily, I say unto you, I know you not" (Matthew 25:12).

Pretense means nothing; God is not a fool. Having the look of a Christian does not make us one. We might talk about God, go to a church, wear Scripture on our clothes, but we need to ask ourselves: if we are true women of God, do we exalt Him with our thoughts and glorify Him with our actions? Are we chaste in spirit?

*Sow to yourselves in righteousness, reap in mercy; break
up your fallow ground: for it is time to seek the Lord, till
he come and rain righteousness upon you. (Hosea 10:12)*

Every one of us has fallow ground. Areas of paltry spiritual
growth, rock-hard earth we've neglected to break up out of
fear or laziness, like not readily submitting to our husbands, or
opening our homes to hospitality, not having self-control in
spending, or patience with our kids. God knows this and pleads
for us to break it up, to trust Him. Righteousness *will* rain
down. Christ, the gift from above, will infuse our parched land
with His Spirit when we willingly tip up our faces to receive it.

The commands God gave the Israelites were as straightforward to them as they are for us: (a) repent—turn away from
sin and return to God, (b) live by godly love—mercy, kindness,
righteous judgment, and (c) be faithful—stay true to Him until
the end (Hosea 12:6). Hosea is a book of pleading from a perfect
husband who does not want to lose His bride. He wants to
lavish her with mercy, peace, and joy. He wants to see her
arrayed in the splendor of His righteousness and to live as one
with her forever.

# What's the story behind...?

*The princes of Judah were like them that **remove the bound**.*
*(Hosea 5:10)*

These *bounds* were landmarks, usually inscribed stones, designating where a family's property corners started and stopped. Anyone who removed a bound encroached upon someone else's land, stealing what wasn't theirs and taking away that family's inheritance. God specifically warned against this egregious offense in Deuteronomy 19:14 and again in 27:17. By comparing the leaders of Judah to those who would remove the bound, the prophet Hosea showed them where their hearts stood in love to God and love to their neighbors.

# Hosea notes

1. *Strong's* reference H3157.

2. *Strong's* reference H3819.

3. *Strong's* reference H3818.

4. *Strong's* reference H1537, taken from H1536 and H1534.

5. *Strong's* reference H669.

6. "Who are Ephraim, Judah, and Jacob in Hosea 10:11?" Bible Hermeneutics Stack Exchange, April 21, 2021, accessed April 19, 2025, https:// hermeneutics.stackexchange.com/questions/59270/ who-are-ephraim-judah-and-jacob-in-hosea-1011.

7. See Romans 2:28–29; 8:14–17; 9:8; and Galatians 3:7, 26–29.

# Joel

*Fear not ... for the Lord will do great things*

The book of Hosea portrays God as a husband. In the book of Joel, He's the ultimate husbandman. A husbandman is a tiller of the soil who works the land to sow, cultivate, prune, and tend his fields to produce food for his family, his community, and the animals he cares for. His efforts mean life for all.

*I am the true vine, and my Father is the husbandman. . . .*
*I am the vine, ye are the branches: He that abideth in me,*
*and I in him, the same bringeth forth much fruit: for*
*without me ye can do nothing. (John 15:1, 5)*

The prophet Joel began his prophecy with a stark declaration for the Israelites that their land would soon be ravaged by an adversary stronger than they'd ever known. This "northern army" (Joel 2:20)—the Assyrians for Joel's audience, but also a future end-times army referred to in Jeremiah, Ezekiel, and Revelation—brought destruction to the land and devastation of everything joyful to the people of Israel. After generations of falsehood and idolatry, God allowed this adversary to run rampant as punishment for Israel's unfaithfulness.

Ancient Israel was an agricultural society that relied upon the land for everything. We modern people are no longer strictly agricultural, but even in our high-tech era, if the land suffers, everything and everyone will suffer along with it because our sustenance still depends upon what the earth provides. The three main crops grown in ancient Israel were grains (mostly wheat and barley), grapes, and olives for precious olive oil. Other produce of the land mentioned in Joel were fruit trees like the fig, pomegranate, (date) palm, and apple.

The analogy Joel used in chapter 1 of an invasion of predatory insects, one after the other successively stripping the land bare, would strike terror in the people fearful of starvation. It would panic the priests as well who needed the grain, oil, and wine produced by the land for the daily meat offering, which was bread made from flour, oil, and frankincense,[1] and the daily drink offering made from wine crucial for proper worship of God. These daily sacrifices were part of the Hebrew culture and a necessary part of the sacred service of the priests. The offerings were an expression of gratitude to God for His blessings and for their standing with Him. Because of Israel's conduct as a nation, the cessation of the agricultural products they needed by the razing of this army was a direct result of God's displeasure and withholding of blessing (Joel 1:13). God allows affliction as a wake-up call. Nothing stirs a soul more than to take away their daily food. "Is not the meat cut off before our eyes, yea, joy and gladness from the house of our God?" (Joel 1:16).

## Repetition

When we repeat ourselves in conversation (think mothers talking to their children), we are emphasizing the importance of our words. Repetition is a means of getting someone's attention and hoping they will hear us and do what we ask. God's Word uses the same method. There are four similar phrases that are repeated in Joel that the children of God needed to heed.

1. Lament and gird yourselves with sackcloth (1:8, 13). That is, humble yourselves. Grieve your faithless actions and cry unto God for mercy.
2. Sanctify a fast (1:14; 2:15). That is, stop entertaining yourselves with food, drink, or anything else. Proclaim a time for God alone.
3. Call a solemn assembly (1:14; 2:15). That is, bring everyone together, young and old. Your recklessness affects whole families.
4. Blow ye the trumpet (2:1, 15). That is, stop what you're doing right now. This is serious; a calamity of your making is approaching.

Fasting is a physical act that produces spiritual gains. When we voluntarily give up our daily food (or anything else we hold dear) for a time, it disciplines our bodies and sharpens our minds toward greater clarity and worship of God. "Blessed are they which do hunger and thirst after righteousness: for they shall be filled" (Matthew 5:6). Fasting's main purpose is to remind us accutely that God is our source of sustenance and strength. As we deprive ourselves of the pleasure of food and drink in a spirit of humility, our spiritual man grows stronger and our hearing of God more acute. Important decisions, the overcoming of sins, and closeness to God are better achieved through fasting and prayer. And this is what God demanded the people of Joel's time to do while they still could.

## The prophecies of Joel

All the books of the Major Prophets and most of the Minor Prophets speak of (a) present-day events declared by that prophet for the people living at that time, (b) future events foreseen by that prophet for that generation's future or for future generations, i.e., modern times, and (c) literal and figurative language used to describe the final end-time days of the wrath of God and Christ's second coming. The book of Joel speaks of all three.

> *And it shall come to pass afterward, that I will pour out my spirit upon all flesh; and your sons and your daughters shall prophesy, your old men shall dream dreams, your young men shall see visions. (Joel 2:28)*

God's Spirit was not always accessible as it is now. Only a select few in biblical times were breathed upon with godly understanding. But ever since Christ's sacrifice—the "afterward" in Joel 2:28—the veil of separation was torn asunder and direct access to the Father was granted to believers. What a glorious gift to be filled with the Spirit of God! Believe it or not, the phrase "your daughters shall prophesy," applies to you and me. To prophesy is not merely predicting future events, but speaking words of wisdom, basic day-to-day discourse from a godly perspective.

- When you lift up your sisters with the truth of God's Word, you prophesy.
- When you humbly share your biblical knowledge in love, you prophesy.
- When you point to our future hope in Christ and His kingdom, you prophesy.

God's Spirit gives us women the power to overcome our sins, to build our faith, to bless others with comfort and encouragement, and to live victoriously in this world no matter our circumstances. And when we speak to others about what God has done for us and within us, when we share the hope of Christ with thanksgiving and joy, as Anna did in Luke 2:38, we prophesy.

The apostle Peter quoted Joel 2:28–32 almost word for word in Acts 2:17–21. Because the book of Joel was part of the holy Scriptures Peter read in his day, he saw the fulfillment of those oft-read Scriptures firsthand after Christ's resurrection when God poured out His Spirit like a mighty wind to the faithful gathered in Jerusalem. Peter was also a witness to Christ's words concerning the end times recorded in Matthew 24 and Luke 21 and remembered what he read in Joel when he spoke to the men of Jerusalem of what was yet to come.

*And I will shew wonders in heaven above, and signs in the earth beneath; blood, and fire, and vapour of smoke. (Acts 2:19)*

*The sun shall be turned into darkness, and the moon into*
*blood, before that great and notable day of the Lord come.*
*(Acts 2:20)*

## End-Times Parallels between Old and New Testaments

In Revelation chapter 9, the apostle John described an "army of horseman" closely resembling the army described in Joel chapter 2. John's vision showed this great tribulation army ascending through thick smoke from the bottomless pit as locusts likened to horses prepared for war, "and the sound of their wings was as the sound of chariots of many horses running to battle" (Revelation 9:9). Joel described these same events as "a day of darkness and of gloominess, a day of clouds and of thick darkness" when this end-time army more powerful than "there hath not been ever the like, neither shall be any more after it" would come "as horsemen, so shall they run. Like the noise of chariots on the tops of mountains shall they leap" (Joel 2:2–5).

Here is another Joel–Revelation parallel: "The earth shall quake before them; the heavens shall tremble; the sun and the moon shall be dark, and the stars shall withdraw their shining" (Joel 2:10; 3:15). In Revelation it reads: "And I beheld when he had opened the sixth seal, and, lo, there was a great earthquake; and the sun became black as sackcloth of hair, and the moon became as blood; And the stars of heaven fell unto the earth" (Revelation 6:12–13).

And in Matthew, the author spoke of the end times similarly: "Immediately after the tribulation of those days shall the sun be darkened, and the moon shall not give her light, and the stars shall fall from heaven, and the powers of the heavens shall be shaken." These three instances in the books of Joel, Matthew, and Revelation all have the same elements: the sun and the moon go dark, stars fall, the heavens are shaken, and the tribes mourn when Christ returns to judge the nations and to gather His saints (Matthew 24:31). All the tribes mourn and wail (Revelation 1:7) because they have refused to believe, and now their judgment from a righteous God is at hand.

| Events Recorded | Joel | Matthew | Revelation |
|---|---|---|---|
| Army of horsemen | Joel 2:4 | —————— | Revelation 9:9 |
| Sound of chariots | Joel 2:5 | —————— | Revelation 9:9 |
| A time/ enemy like no other | Joel 2:2 | Matthew 24:21 | —————— |
| Great earthquake | Joel 2:10 | Matthew 24:7 | Revelation 6:12 |
| Heavens shaken/ tremble | Joel 2:10; 3:15 | Matthew 24:29 | Revelation 6:12 |
| Sun and moon dark | Joel 2:10; 3:15 | Matthew 24:29 | Revelation 6:12 |
| Stars fall/ withdraw | Joel 2:10 | Matthew 24:29 | Revelation 6:13 |

| Events Recorded | Joel | Matthew | Revelation |
|---|---|---|---|
| Tribes mourn/ pained | Joel 2:6 | Matthew 24:30 | Revelation 1:7 |
| Christ returns/the day of the Lord | Joel 2:11; 3:16 | Matthew 24:30–31 | Revelation 19:11–16 |

Here is a simplified sequence of events of the end times:

1.  The majority of the world embraces an anti-God, one-world government or New World Order called "the beast" for seven years (Revelation 13:1–6).

2.  Three-and-a-half years into this seven-year period begins the great tribulation when the beast will make war with the saints [God's children] (Revelation 12:17), denying them the power to buy and sell (Revelation 13:17), killing those who refuse to worship the image of the beast (Revelation 13:15), and ultimately over-coming many of them (Revelation 13:7; Daniel 7:21).

3.  Christ, the Almighty (Revelation 1:8), returns at the seventh trumpet at the end of the tribulation (1 Thessalonians 4:16; Revelation 11:15), and the dead in Christ rise first (1 Thessalonians 4:16; 1 Corinthians 15:51–52), then all who still remain, all who belong to Christ, will be instantly changed from mortal into immortal, from physical bodies to spiritual bodies,

and meet Him in the air,[2] and forever be with Him (1 Thessalonians 4:17).

4. Meanwhile, the heathen (those who refuse Christ) are subject to the seven last plagues of the wrath of God. They refuse to repent and instead band together at a place called Armageddon,[3] the valley of decision, to fight with the Almighty and His angels and are soundly defeated (Joel 3:11–14; Revelation 17:14; 19:19–20).

5. With evil gone, the millennium on earth begins for the remaining uncalled physical human beings who did not fight against Christ at Armageddon.[4] Without Satan's influence for a thousand years, they will learn the wisdom of God unhindered and see in the resurrected and recently changed spirit beings the reward that obeying God gives. Peace on earth is finally a reality.[5]

## Jehoshaphat and the valley of decision

In 2 Chronicles 20, we read an account of the Israelites up against a fierce enemy. Jehoshaphat, the king of Judah, was greatly outnumbered by this approaching army, but the prophet Jahaziel, filled with the Spirit of God, told him and all the people, "Be not afraid, nor dismayed by reason of this great multitude; for the battle is not yours, but God's" (2 Chronicles 20:15). While all the people sang praises to the Lord, He fought their enemy, and not one of them escaped. This was the valley of Jehoshaphat, the valley of decision,[6] that was spoken of in Joel chapter 3 about the days to come. Future nations who will not repent will be bent on fighting God and will "beat [their] plowshares into swords, and [their] pruninghooks into spears" (Joel 3:10).

> *Let the heathen be awakened, and come up to the valley of Jehoshaphat. . . .*
> *Multitudes, multitudes in the valley of decision; for the day of the Lord is near in the valley of decision. (Joel 3:12, 14)*

As was mentioned in the commentary on Hosea, whenever we read the phrase "the day of the Lord," this signifies the end-times judgment of unbelievers and the second coming of Christ. "The day of the Lord" is repeated four times in Joel.

> *And the Lord shall utter his voice before his army: for his camp is very great: for he is strong that executeth his word: for the day of the Lord is great and very terrible; and who can abide it? (Joel 2:11)*

Directly after this verse, we are told how to survive or abide this desperate time—turn to God with all our hearts. With fasting, weeping, and mourning, realize our great need for God.

> *And rend your heart, and not your garments, and turn unto the Lord your God: for he is gracious and merciful, slow to anger, and of great kindness, and repenteth him of the evil. (Joel 2:13)*

When we surrender our lives to God, we become His. When we put our faith in Christ daily, we no longer have to fear the wrath of God to come. But we must stay vigilant. Watching and praying always that we "may be accounted worthy to escape all these things that shall come to pass, and to stand before the Son of man" (Luke 21:36).

*And it shall come to pass, that whosoever shall call on the name of the Lord shall be delivered: **for in mount Zion and in Jerusalem shall be deliverance,** as the Lord hath said, and in the remnant whom the Lord shall call.*
*(Joel 2:32, emphasis added)*

In Romans 10:13, Paul quoted Joel when he wrote, "For whosoever shall call upon the name of the Lord shall be saved." Joel declared mount Zion and the city of Jerusalem holy places where our deliverance is found. Christ is our mount Zion, He is our Jerusalem. Whether we live or die during the end times, our spiritual deliverance is assured. But God wanted the Israelites in Joel's time and for us in ours to "rend your heart, and not your garments" (Joel 2:13). Yes, God promises to be merciful to us in His "great and terrible day," but He is not fooled by the outward look of a Christian. He wants genuine inner change and true repentance as it is spoken of in Psalm 34:18, "The Lord is nigh [near] unto them that are of a broken heart; and saveth such as be of a contrite spirit." With a shout and a trumpet call, Christ ushers in the millennium, His thousand-year period of true peace and prosperity, to those who are His.

The chart on the following page shows the prophecies recorded in the book of Joel are the same prophecies found in several New Testament books.

| Joel<br><br>Both verses on the right come after the sun and the moon have become dark. This helps us better understand the timeline of events when Christ returns. | *The Lord shall **utter his voice** before his army. (Joel 2:11)*<br><br>*The Lord also **shall roar** out of Zion, and utter his voice from Jerusalem. (Joel 3:16)* |
|---|---|
| 1 Thessalonians | *For the Lord himself shall descend from heaven **with a shout**, with the **voice of the archangel**, and with the **trump of God**: and the dead in Christ shall rise first. (1 Thessalonians 4:16)* |
| Matthew | *And he shall send his angels with a great **sound of a trumpet**, and they shall gather together his elect from the four winds, from one end of heaven to the other. (Matthew 24:31)* |
| 1 Corinthians | *In a moment, in the twinkling of an eye, at the last trump: for the **trumpet shall sound**, and the dead shall be raised incorruptible, and we shall be changed. (1 Corinthians 15:52)* |
| Revelation | *And the seventh **angel sounded**; and there were **great voices** in heaven, saying, The kingdoms of this world are become the kingdoms of our Lord, and of his Christ; and he shall reign for ever and ever. (Revelation 11:15)* |

The book of Joel provides us with much to ponder and prepare for. We, as women of God, can be confident that when Christ returns He will "restore to you the years that the locust hath eaten . . . and ye shall eat in plenty, and be satisfied, and praise the name of the Lord your God, that hath dealt wondrously with you: and my people shall never be ashamed" (Joel 2:25–26). We all have lost something from the locusts of hardship, betrayal, sickness, pain, and fear. Our lives here are imperfect and wanting. But what if *we* were the locusts? What if it was our rebellion to God from our past that brought about the damage and sorrows, the ragged holes in our lives we still regret? Even if this is true, God's promise still stands. God, in all His unfathomable mercy, will exchange our locust-losses, self-inflicted or not, with healing and wholeness. He will deal wondrously with us.

# What's the story behind...?

*Before the face the people shall be much pained: all faces*
**shall gather blackness.** *(Joel 2:6)*

The word *blackness* used here and in Nahum 2:10 was most likely a reference to what the face and body looked like when covered in ashes during mourning. But blackness is also meant as a figurative flush of anxiety,[7] a spiritual darkness one would feel when all hope is lost and physical destruction is imminent.[8]

## Joel notes

1. See Leviticus 2:2.
2. We meet Christ in the air, but that doesn't mean we stay in the air. God is descending from heaven to be with us on earth. God's kingdom will be on this earth, and we will reign with Christ here as spirit beings (Revelation 5:10). See also Daniel 7:27; Zechariah 14:9; Matthew 5:5; 1 Corinthians 6:1–3; and Revelation 1:6; 11:15.
3. *Strong's* reference G717, taken from H2022: *mountain* or *range of hills*, H4023: *rendezvous*, and H1413: *gather selves in troops*. See also BibleFocus.net, "Armageddon and the Valley of Jehoshaphat," September 27, 2005, accessed on April 19, 2025, https://biblefocus.net/consider/v01Armageddon/Armageddon-To-Occur-In-The-Valley-of.html.
4. While not conclusive, the Bible infers there will be "nations" left to teach, govern, and judge during the millennium when we reign with Christ (Matthew 19:28; 1 Corinthians 6:2; Revelation 20:3). But this could also refer to right after the millennium when billions are resurrected in the second resurrection.
5. There is more to the story. Since none of the twelve books of the Minor Prophets refers to the timeline after the millennium, please read Revelation chapter 20 to learn about Satan's release from his bonds after the thousand years are finished, his deceiving the nations (again!), the great white throne judgment, and the second death.

6. *Strong's* reference H2742: *incised, trench* (as dug) *threshing instrument,* (figuratively) *determination.*

7. *Strong's* reference H6289.

8. See also Jeremiah 8:21.

# Amos

*Seek the Lord and you shall live*

From the humble fields of Tekoa, south of Jerusalem, God called Amos to wield the rod of correction on His unruly flock. But the people would have none of it. Amos's presence and pronouncements were an offense to them. The religious rulers of the day were living in a delusion of their own grandeur and righteousness. How dare this lowly shepherd utter his voice against us! Amos was one of many prophets who bore the burden of warning the complacent and compromised Israelites. In fact, the name *Amos* means "burden, or burden-bearer."[1] The local priest intimidated him and told him to leave. Amos was disturbing their manufactured peace.

Amos didn't ask for this job. He didn't come from a line of prophets nor was he the son of a prophet. He was a simple herdsman and picker of fruit, but God picked him. And he obeyed. "The lion hath roared, who will not fear? the Lord God hath spoken, who can but prophesy?" (Amos 3:8). The world hates truth and those that dare to speak it. This was true for Amos and is equally true for us. Even in America, a nation founded on godly principles, decency has been dethroned, the Bible is picked apart, and hearts have turned to stone. Theories are touted as facts and laws are rewritten to placate the conscience of the masses.

Like unwelcomed Amos, truth is unwelcome in every area of our society. We are surrounded by a broadcast of lies, and those that entertain and inform us live in their self-made world where falsehood is their native tongue. Where murder conjures indifference, not shock. Depravity draws delight, not shame. Where civility rots on the plate while hatred is gorged as a honeycomb. For they have turned "judgment into gall, and the fruit of righteousness into hemlock" (Amos 6:12).

If you, as a woman of God, utter the voice of reason, if you utter the wisdom that comes from above, hatred and derision will come. A wife and mother who chooses to submit to her husband, honor her marriage vows, and teach her own children will get ridicule and pushback from the world. But no matter how many gather together and shout their consensus against you and God's truth, they will not prevail. "Though hand join in hand, the wicked shall not be unpunished: but the seed of the righteous shall be delivered" (Proverbs 11:21).

In the book of Amos, there are poetic patterns of repetition in which God speaks against the wickedness of Israel's six neighboring nations: Damascus, Gaza, Edom, Tyrus, Ammon, and Moab, ending with the sins of Judah and Israel. "For three transgressions, and for four" these nations' sins were not forgotten.

God remembered how they treated Israel and each other and declared what would befall them. Although the nations of Israel and Judah were set apart by God—"You only have I known of all the families of the earth" (Amos 3:2)—their sins were often worse than the Gentile nations around them.

*For I know your manifold transgressions and your mighty sins: they afflict the just, they take a bribe, and they turn aside the poor in the gate from their right. (Amos 5:12)*

God raised up prophets for the good of Israel. But the people refused to listen and commanded the prophets to stop speaking. He gave them a blueprint of conduct they crumpled like junk mail eager to commit fornication and adultery, sacrifice their own children as other nations did, and live by deceitful gain and the lies of their fathers. Israel was not walking with God and God had had enough. "Can two walk together, except they be agreed?" (Amos 3:3).

Because Israel stored up violence and robbery in her palaces (Amos 3:10), served pagan gods like Moloch and Chiun (Amos 5:26), and dealt deceitfully with the poor for their own gain (Amos 8:5–6), God was sending an adversary to bring her down and drag her from her land. Israel would be devoured like the prey of a lion. As a shepherd takes out bits and pieces of his flock from the mouth of a lion, only a remnant of Israel would escape (Amos 3:12). And only because of God's tremendous mercy did He promise "I will not utterly destroy the house of Jacob" (Amos 9:8).

## God never does evil

Satan is the author of all things evil. He takes what is good and turns it into death and decay. The King James Bible translators, however, had a hard time translating certain words with complex meanings from the Hebrew and Greek languages into English. The word *evil* was one of them.

> *Shall a trumpet be blown in the city, and the people not be afraid? Shall there be evil in a city, and the Lord hath not done it? (Amos 3:6)*

> *And though they go into captivity before their enemies, thence will I command the sword, and it shall slay them: and I will set mine eyes upon them for evil, and not for good. (Amos 9:3)*

In these verses above, *evil* means "adversity, calamity, or affliction."[2] God withdrew His hand of blessing from the Israelites by allowing war, pestilence, hunger, drought, and crop failures, and even with all that, "yet have ye not returned unto me, saith the Lord" (Amos 4:6–11). God brings affliction to the unrepentant. He allows distress to vex those who refuse to change. And sometimes, as in Job 2:10 and 42:11, God permits suffering to test the character of His children. But God never creates evil.

King Saul was one of a few people in the Old Testament that God gave of His Spirit, but because of Saul's disobedience, it was taken away. In 1 Samuel 16:14, the text reads that when the Spirit of God departed from Saul "an evil spirit from the Lord troubled him." Since we know evil doesn't come from God, the answer to this confusion in translation is Saul experienced a spirit of torment, a debilitating depression, and a deeply troubled conscience directly related to his disobedience to God. God is the author of good. Nothing good comes to us except through God. And if we ever depart from the wisdom and righteousness of God, we can expect nothing but the opposite of good: adversity, calamity, and affliction.

## The significance of Bethel and Gilgal

Bethel was originally a sacred and holy place where God spoke to Jacob while he dreamed upon his stone pillow. This was the place God blessed Jacob and his future seed and changed his name to Israel. But many years later, the Israelites sinned greatly at Bethel. It was there that Judah's king Jeroboam made two golden calves for worship. He set one in Bethel and the other in Dan and appointed priests, not of the sons of Levi as God had instructed from the beginning, to oversee their worship. Jeroboam ordained a feast day of his own devising and said, "Behold thy gods, O Israel, which brought thee up out of the land of Egypt" (1 Kings 12:28).

> *For this saith the Lord unto the house of Israel, Seek ye me, and ye shall live:*
> *But seek not Bethel, nor enter into Gilgal, and pass not to Beersheba: for Gilgal shall surely go into captivity, and Bethel shall come to nought. (Amos 5:4–5)*

The Israelites took the elements of the earth, elements they could manipulate and mold, and replaced the true God. They took the Maker of all things and reduced Him to something they could control. That is true of today's churches. There are many "Bethels" bringing in abominable heresies because it's what the masses want. They'd rather have something shiny and man-made than to behold—and be held accountable to—an uncontrollable God.

Gilgal (as mentioned in Hosea) had a similar history with Bethel. It was a sacred place dedicated to God, but had become tainted and entirely devoid of righteousness. With this in mind, we can see why God warned the Israelites to seek not Bethel nor enter into Gilgal. They had completely corrupted these places, making a mockery of worship and polluting that which was sacred. He wanted no more of it.

## Christians at ease

> *Woe to them that are at ease in Zion, and trust in the mountain of Samaria, which are named chief of the nations, to whom the house of Israel came! ...*
> *Ye that put far away the evil day, and cause the seat of violence to come near. (Amos 6:1, 3)*

The "evil day" was this very prophecy of their destruction. The warning that Amos delivered they put far into the future thinking surely it was not for them to heed now. But, oh, they were wrong. God gave His people a choice before their destruction when He said, "Hate the evil, and love the good, and establish judgment in the gate: it may be that the Lord God of hosts will be gracious unto the remnant of Joseph" (Amos 5:15). God pleaded with His children to consider who He was and to "seek good, and not evil, that ye may live" (Amos 5:14). He pleaded with them to seek the God who made Orion and Pleiades, constellations they had named and chosen to worship instead,[3] to seek the God who turns the shadow of death into the morning, pours the waters of the sea onto the face of the earth, and strengthens the weak against the strong (Amos 5:8–9).

> *For, lo, he that formeth the mountains, and createth the wind, and declareth unto man what is his thought, that maketh the morning darkness, and treadeth upon the high places of the earth, The Lord, The God of hosts, is his name. (Amos 4:13)*

Throughout Israel's history, God chose prophets to speak His plans, His secret counsel to the people (Amos 3:7). But the people, as Amos recorded, were more concerned with leisure and with keeping things as they were than with honoring God (Amos 6:4–6). They believed, like many people do today, that by their own strength they produced the good in their lives (Amos 6:13). All the opulence of their lifestyle and the feigned observance of their holy days and the melody of their songs God hated (Amos 5:21; Isaiah 1:14–18). And along came Amos to let them know it.

Long before Amos and straight to the present, worldly people confronted by their sins have despised righteous truth and those who speak it.

> [They] *make a man an offender for a word, and lay a snare for him that reproveth in the gate, and turn aside the just for a thing of nought. (Isaiah 29:21)*

*They hate him that rebuketh in the gate, and they abhor*
*him that speaketh uprightly. (Amos 5:10)*

It takes a humble spirit to accept correction and to listen to
the uncomfortable truth that we need to overcome our faults.
But our human nature often bristles when confronted, points
fingers at the one speaking, and prefers the come-as-you-are,
stay-as-you-are lie. God wants you to come as you are, yes. But
stay as you are—never. Many people sitting in churches today
think they are heaven-bound. They've chosen to listen to
leaders who hold hands with the world and tell their
congregation they are good enough the way they are. And
because of this nonsense, they don't grow spiritually at all.
These shepherds send them home deluded. But what has God
said? "Woe unto you that desire the day of the Lord! To what
end is it for you? The day of the Lord is darkness, and not light"
(Amos 5:18).

For many, the end times or the *day of the Lord* won't be
what they hoped, because they refuse to heed the warnings and
repent, as the Israelites had refused in Amos's day. Like a basket
of summer fruit, we are picked and ripe for repentance or on
the verge of decay (Amos 8:1–2). It's either one or the other.
For those who profess Christ, the time is now. But as people
continue in their self-deception, God's Word will become
scarce in their minds. They will reach for it less and less because
it disturbs their lifestyle.

*Behold, the days come, saith the Lord God, that I will send*
*a famine in the land, not a famine of bread, not a thirst for*
*water, but of hearing the words of the Lord. (Amos 8:11)*

Paul spoke in 2 Timothy 4:3–4 about those who no longer would listen to sound doctrine but prefer to hear what didn't offend them. Let that never be us. Let us always compare what we hear from others to what is actually written in God's Word.

Throughout the Bible, God deals with the unrepentant and forewarns any who will listen. Judgment will come, but He mercifully gives us a way out of our self-inflicted doom. When we choose God's will over our own, He promises a coming kingdom of restitution and plenty.

*Behold, the days come, saith the Lord, that the plowman shall overtake the reaper, and the treader of grapes him that soweth seed; and the mountains shall drop sweet wine, and all the hills shall melt. (Amos 9:13)*

When we obey God now, we will be unable to contain the blessings of the future, there will be so many. In the book of Amos, God speaks His words of life to those who will hear. He even speaks of the hope of salvation for the future Gentiles who will call on His name.[4] He wants us to judge between right and wrong without making excuses and to love others while upholding His truth. He wants us to let "judgment run down as waters, and righteousness as a mighty stream" (Amos 5:24). And if we are filled with His Spirit, we can and we will.

## What's the story behind...?

*I have overthrown some of you, as God overthrew Sodom and Gomorrah, and ye were as a **firebrand** plucked out of the burning: yet have ye not returned unto me, saith the Lord. (Amos 4:11)*

Firebrands were objects meant for the fire. They were either sticks used to stir a fire or wooden torches with burning and blackened ends. They may have also been fiery darts used in warfare.

God told the children of Israel and Judah that they were living as if they already resided in hell, and by the kindness and mercy of God, He snatched them out of that fire of destruction, yet they still didn't humble themselves or show gratitude.

Two similar phrases are found in Zechariah 3:2, "Is not this a brand plucked out of the fire?" and in Jude 1:23, "And others save with fear, pulling them out of the fire." Many people are destined for hellfire. They won't accept God's goodness or help from others. But for those who are willing, your loving, yet fearful reminder of where their actions are leading them could make all the difference in their final destination.

## Amos notes

1. *Strong's* reference H5986: *burdensome*; taken from H6006; *to load, impose a burden.*
2. *Strong's* reference H7451.
3. The martyr Stephen quoted Amos 5:25 in the book of Acts when confronted and accused by the angry members of the synagogue. "Then God turned, and gave them up to worship the host of heaven; as it is written in the book of the prophets, O ye house of Israel, have ye offered to me slain beasts and sacrifices by the space of forty years in the wilderness?" (Acts 7:42).
4. The apostle James quoted Amos 9:11–12 to the gathering of apostles and elders recorded in Jerusalem in Acts 15:16–17.

# Obadiah

*As thou hast done, it shall be done unto thee*

Not much is known about the prophet Obadiah. But his name means *servant of the Lord*,[1] so we know he was obedient to his calling as a prophet. He was known by God and that is what matters most. The book of Obadiah is the shortest book in the Old Testament and concerns the judgment of Edom. The nation of Edom descended from Jacob's twin brother, Esau. In Obadiah we read how jealousy, hatred, and pride consumed a nation. These bitter emotions can lodge in our womanly hearts too, hurting those around us for generations if we allow our circumstances to dictate how we act and how we think.

Most of us are familiar with the story in Genesis chapter 25. Esau, desperately hungry, willingly gave up his inheritance to his brother, Jacob, for a bowl of soup. He did not regard his status as the firstborn with respect (was it too much of a burden?) and was more concerned with his present than with his future. Later, when he would have inherited his portion, it was unreachable, and he bewailed his hasty decision. We've all been there, haven't we? Been more concerned with our feelings at the moment than with how the fulfillment of our desires will affect our future. Mistakes and their consequences cannot be separated. We may not feel the impact of our wrong choices right away, but it will come, and we will have to live with it like Esau with his woeful regrets.

Although Esau was rejected as the firstborn, God did not entirely forget Esau but gave him and his people Mount Seir for a possession (Deuteronomy 2:5). Hundreds of years later, when the children of Israel plodded through the wilderness after God brought them out of Egypt, He commanded them not to meddle with Esau, not to think about possessing any part of their land, and specifically, not to abhor an Edomite (Deuteronomy 23:7). God showed Edom compassion. Yet for all that, Obadiah verse 5 describes Edom as not having the compassion of robbers, to steal only as much as they could carry or to gather grapes and drop a few for others. Edom was as heartless as that.

> *The pride of thine heart hath deceived thee, thou that dwellest in the clefts of the rock, whose habitation is high; that saith in his heart, Who shall bring me down to the ground? (Obadiah 3)*

Mountains are strategic strongholds in times of war. Being able to look down and see what's coming gives you the advantage. But a physical advantage won't save anyone if God says otherwise, neither will physical wealth. Pride, the opposite of humility, is an insidious sin. Pride turned Lucifer into Satan. He placed the glory of his beauty and accomplishments on himself, not where it rightfully belonged—upon Almighty God. And Edom fell to this same sickness. "How are the things of Esau searched out! how are his hidden things sought up!" (Obadiah 6). Pride, jealousy, and hatred: Edom could not hide them from God.

## The story of Jacob and Esau

Where did the resentment and hatred come from that Edom harbored against Israel? How did it all begin?

> For the children being not yet born, neither having done any good or evil, that the purpose of God according to election might stand, not of works, but of him that calleth;
> It was said unto her, The elder shall serve the younger.
> As it is written, Jacob have I loved, but Esau have I hated. (Romans 9:11–13)

Hatred for Jacob consumed Esau after his younger brother deceived their nearly blind father, Isaac, into giving Jacob the blessing of the firstborn instead of him. Look at all the negative emotions and repercussions stemming from the players of this story that spilled onto the next generation. Human nature at its worst.

- jealousy (Esau; Rachel, and Leah, Jacob's two wives)
- deception and lying (Jacob and Rebekah, his mother; Laban, Jacob's father-in-law)

- anger and hatred (Esau)
- favoritism (Isaac and Rebekah, parents of Esau and Jacob; Jacob toward his wives)
- spite (Esau, purposely marrying a heathen woman)
- envy (Esau and Rachel)
- one-upmanship (Rachel and Leah, sisters)

Esau resented Jacob for the divine favor God extended to his brother. Later, the nation of Edom acted upon that resentment. Have you ever felt resentment toward a brother or sister in Christ because of their perceived favor with God? Have they been blessed with the blessings you seek but do not have?

> *Follow peace with all men, and holiness, without which no man shall see the Lord:*
> *Looking diligently lest any man fail of the grace of God; lest any root of bitterness springing up trouble you, and thereby many be defiled;*
> *Lest there be any fornicator, or profane person, as Esau, who for one morsel of meat sold his birthright.*
> *For ye know how that afterward, when he would have inherited the blessing, he was rejected: for he found no place of repentance, though he sought it carefully with tears. (Hebrews 12:14–17)*

The name *Jacob* means "supplanter" or "heel-catcher" in Hebrew.[2] To supplant means to *circumvent* or *restrain*. Jacob was chosen by God from the time he was in Rebekah's womb to take the birthright from Esau. But God did not need Rebekah or her son, Jacob, to deceive Isaac to make that happen. Like Sarai's impatience to conceive led her to make a grave mistake and rush things by handing over her handmaid, Hagar, to Abram,[3] how often do we step in and try to make something happen ahead of God only to make things much, much worse? The bitterness that started with Esau never left the nation of Edom. In Numbers 20:18–21, we learn this in a gruesome way.

When King Saul lost favor with God for his disobedience, he sought to kill his successor, David. David fled the anger of Saul and sought refuge among the priests in Jerusalem as well as the neighboring city of Nob. King Saul commanded his personal servants to kill everyone who aided David. He ordered the slaughter of all the priests of God, but his servants wisely disobeyed the king's command for their greater fear of God. Saul, however, had in his employ a wicked man named Doeg, an Edomite, who had no problem with Saul's command and went forth and killed eighty-five priests and the entire city of Nob that gave safe harbor to David, including women and children. God never forgot that treachery.

> *Because thou hast had a perpetual hatred, and hast shed the blood of the children of Israel by the force of the sword in the time of their calamity, in the time that their iniquity had an end:*
> *Therefore, as I live, saith the Lord God, I will prepare thee unto blood, and blood shall pursue thee: sith thou hast not hated blood, even blood shall pursue thee. (Ezekiel 35:5–6)*

Jesus Christ taught in Matthew 7:12 and Luke 6:31 that we should treat others as we would want them to treat us. This is akin to the second greatest commandment He taught that we love our neighbors as ourselves. Edom was a brother to Israel but didn't treat him like a brother. Instead, Edom watched as the southern kingdom of Israel (Judah) was attacked, plundered, and carried away from their land by the Babylonians. Their inaction turned to action as they took part in their brother's spoiling and destruction.

> *Remember, O Lord, the children of Edom in the day of Jerusalem; who said, Rase it, rase it, even to the foundation thereof. (Psalm 137:7)*

They rejoiced over Israel's demise and proudly made it known. They even captured those trying to escape and turned them over to Israel's enemy (Obadiah 12). But God declared, "As thou hast done; it shall be done unto thee: thy reward shall return upon thine own head" (Obadiah 15). God is the God of recompenses,[4] and He did not forget Edom's treachery. He promised that no one would remain from the house of Esau (Obadiah 18).

> *Thus saith the Lord; For three transgressions of Edom, and for four, I will not turn away the punishment thereof; because he did pursue his brother with the sword, and did cast off all pity, and his anger did tear perpetually, and he kept his wrath for ever. (Amos 1:11)*

Obadiah wasn't the only prophet of old to speak against Edom. Jeremiah 49:7–22 is an almost word-for-word pronouncement against Edom that is found throughout this one chapter book of Obadiah. The prophets Ezekiel, Amos, and Malachi, also prophesied against Edom. Bible historians have noted that Edom as a nation no longer existed by the first century.[5] God meant what He said. Nothing would remain of the house of Esau.

*Thus saith the Lord God; Because that Edom hath dealt against the house of Judah by taking vengeance, and hath greatly offended, and revenged himself upon them;*
*Therefore thus saith the Lord God; I will also stretch out mine hand upon Edom, and will cut off man and beast from it; and I will make it desolate from Teman;[6] and they of Dedan shall fall by the sword. (Ezekiel 25:12–13)*

God tells us in Proverbs 24:17 not to rejoice over the downfall of anyone. This includes our Christian brothers and sisters. Every one of us has sinful proclivities we need to overcome. No one is perfect. Yet, when we see someone from the Christian community, someone in a high-profile position who's clearly sinned, it can be selfishly gratifying to see them humbled. Paul warned in Romans 11:18–22 not to glory in the downfall of others, lest we fall too. Do not glory, but instead pity. Because one day the openly wicked and those who refuse to repent, even so-called Christians, will be eternally separated from God's love and light. There will be weeping and gnashing of teeth (Matthew 8:12). Weeping of regret for their refusal to heed the Almighty. Gnashing of teeth for the gruesome finality of their choice.

It's human nature to express glee when those who promote evil like pedophiles and mass murderers are taken out of the way. We applaud for the sake of the innocent. When love and truth trump hate and evil, it's a very good thing and should be applauded. But there is a difference between how we respond to the works of the children of wrath and the children themselves. Every single one of us has a choice, and God is exceedingly patient (for He is not willing that any should perish[7]), but there will come a time when He will say, "He that is unjust, let him be unjust still . . . and he that is righteous, let him be righteous still. And, behold, I come quickly; and my reward is with me, to give every man according as his work shall be" (Revelation 22:11–12).

The book of Psalms calls Mount Zion the place where God dwells (Psalm 74:2), and the prophet Obadiah shouted for all to hear: "Upon mount Zion shall be deliverance, and there shall be holiness; and the house of Jacob shall possess their possessions" (Obadiah 17). It is Christ, our savior, who provides a means of escape from our carnal nature and our doomed condition. He is our deliverance.

*And the house of Jacob shall be a fire, and the house of Joseph a flame, and the house of Esau for stubble, and they shall kindle in them, and devour them; and there shall not be any remaining of the house of Esau; for the Lord hath spoken it. (Obadiah 18)*

Christ comes like lightning, the Holy One a flame (Isaiah 10:17) and will devour the thorns to stubble in one day. The thorns of jealousy, hatred, temptation, deceit, resentment, revenge, and pride—everything that drove Edom and ensnares us today—will be wiped out in the last day.

## Our new position as saints

We women have many roles. We are daughters, sisters, aunts, wives, mothers, and friends. Not to mention our varied occupations as homemakers, gardeners, nurses, writers, artists, and businesswomen of all kinds. But someday these earthly roles will dissolve, and we will be saints, and, according to Obadiah, saviors.

> *And saviours shall come up on mount Zion to judge the*
> *mount of Esau; and the kingdom shall be the Lord's.*
> *(Obadiah 21)*

The word *saviours* is found twice in the King James Version. Once in Nehemiah 9:27, meaning to "be safe" or providing "victory," and here in Obadiah, meaning those "having salvation."[8] We are saved by the blood of Christ, and He gives us salvation through faith in His name. Throughout the Bible, Christ says those who overcome will sit on His throne with Him. When Christ judges the nations, we will judge alongside Him because He will give us that authority.[9]

> *And he that overcometh, and keepeth my works unto the*
> *end, to him will I give power over the nations:*
> *And he shall rule them with a rod of iron; as the vessels*
> *of a potter shall they be broken to shivers: even as I*
> *received of my Father. (Revelation 2:26–27)*

> *To him that overcometh will I grant to sit with me in my*
> *throne, even as I also overcame, and am set down with*
> *my Father in his throne. (Revelation 3:21)*

*And hast made us unto our God kings and priests: and*
*we shall reign on the earth. (Revelation 5:10)*

Jesus Christ also spoke to His apostles about their specific role in His kingdom: "And I appoint unto you a kingdom, as my Father hath appointed unto me; That ye may eat and drink at my table in my kingdom, and sit on thrones judging the twelve tribes of Israel" (Luke 22:29–30). Even Paul made it clear to the Corinthian church what our new role as saints would mean. "Do ye not know that the saints shall judge the world? and if the world shall be judged by you, are ye unworthy to judge the smallest matters?" (1 Corinthians 6:2). Prophecy is multifaceted and often obscure, but this we can be certain of: Christ's kingdom is coming to the earth, and we will rule with Him.

*Let the saints be joyful in glory: let them sing aloud*
*upon their beds.*
*Let the high praises of God be in their mouth, and a*
*twoedged sword in their hand;*
*To execute vengeance upon the heathen, and punishments*
*upon the people;*
*To bind their kings with chains, and their nobles with*
*fetters of iron;*
*To execute upon them the judgment written: this honour*
*have all his saints. Praise ye the Lord. (Psalm 149:5–9)*

The book of Obadiah tells the story of Edom's refusal to be humble, loving, and forgiving, and the ultimate retribution they received from God. But Edom's downfall can be traced back to a single family. We women have the power to alter the course of many generations when we refuse to live by anger, resentment, and jealousy and choose sacrificial love and forgiveness instead.

# What's the story behind ...?

*And the captivity of this host of the children of Israel shall
possess that of the Canaanites, even unto **Zarephath**.
(Obadiah 20)*

The Bible mentions Zeraphath in Obadiah verse 20, 1 Kings
17:9–10, and once in Luke 4:26 (spelled *Sarepta* in the Greek).
"But I tell you of a truth, many widows were in Israel in the days
of Elias, when the heaven was shut up three years and six months,
when great famine was throughout all the land; But unto none
of them was Elias [Elijah] sent, save unto Sarepta, a city of Sidon,
unto a woman that was a widow" (Luke 4:25–26).

First Kings recounts the story of the desperate widow
woman living in Zeraphath whom God told the prophet Elijah
to stay with. When Elijah finds her, she is gathering wood to
cook the last of her food for herself and her son. But Elijah asks
her to make her last meal for him without fear because God
would not deplete her food stores. She did not voice doubt or
hesitate, and the three lived off her meager supplies for many
months. Christ told the men in Nazareth this story to rouse
them to shame for their own doubts and attitude of superiority.

# Obadiah notes

1. *Strong's* reference H5662: *serving Jah* (Hebrew for *God*).
2. *Strong's* reference H3290: taken from H6117; to *seize by the heel*.
3. The impatience of Sarai created a whole nest of trouble with the birth of Ishmael, who later became the modern-day Islamic nations. "And he will be a wild man; his hand will be against every man, and every man's hand against him; and he shall dwell in the presence of all his brethren" (Genesis 16:12).
4. *Strong's* reference H1578: *deed, reward*, taken from H1576; *treatment, an act of good or ill, desert* (as in his/her just deserts), *deserving*, by implication *an act of service or requital*. See Jeremiah 51:56.
5. Steve Rudd, "The Edomites" section 4, "Chronology from Edom to Esau to Extinction: 2006 BC–AD 70," The Interactive Bible, accessed April 20, 2025, https://www.bible.ca/archeology/bible-archeology-edomite-territory-mt-seir.htm#IV.
6. Teman, one of Edom's prominent cities, was named after Esau's grandson.
7. See 2 Peter 3:9.
8. *Strong's* reference H3467: to *be open, wide*, or *free*, by implication to *be safe, having salvation, savior, get victory*.
9. See also Daniel 7:27 and Malachi 3:18.

# Jonah

*Salvation is of the Lord*

As Bible stories go, none are more popular than the colorful tales of Jonah and the Big Fish, David and Goliath, and Daniel and the Lion's Den. But these idealized stories told for children often miss the spiritual takeaways and the unsavory parts are left out. If we look closely into the book of Jonah, we will discover a magnificent parallel of God's love and redemption to a multitude of sorrowful people as well as lessons taught to a man who sorrowed for all the wrong reasons. God knows what we're made of and what we need. And Jonah's mission of warning to Nineveh was as much for his own good as it was for theirs.

Have you ever thought of running away from God? Have you squeezed your eyes shut and turned your back on difficult biblical commands? Running away from full obedience to God and all that He's asked us to do is not uncommon. In the first chapter of this book, Jonah did just that.

## The grandeur of Nineveh

Nineveh was a spectacular city in its day, second only to Babylon in size and splendor. The entire circuit of this massive walled city measured seven and a half miles. In the year 1845, archaeologists dug up remains of paved streets and exquisite gates lined with giant winged bulls and lion sphinxes. They unearthed a grand palace flanked by seventy-one halls 40 feet wide and 180 feet long paneled with slabs of sculptured alabaster that recorded the great deeds of the Assyrian kings. These archaeologists also discovered extensive libraries filled with thousands upon thousands of clay tablets, the largest known collection of ancient books on every subject imaginable.[1]

Nineveh, the capital of Assyria, was not only a formidable and awe-inspiring place, it was also Israel's primary enemy at the time. Assyria, during its height of power, was known for its cruelty toward its captives, yet God commanded Jonah to go there anyway and declare to them their need to repent before God destroyed them. Was Jonah scared, hardhearted, or just plain angry to be sent to warn Israel's enemy? We don't know; maybe all three. We do know Jonah didn't say yes to God but tried to hide from Him instead.

*Whither shall I go from thy spirit? or whither shall I flee from thy presence?*
*If I ascend up into heaven, thou art there: if I make my bed in hell, behold, thou art there. (Psalm 139:7–8)*

*Can any hide himself in secret places that I shall not see him? saith the Lord. Do not I fill heaven and earth? saith the Lord. (Jeremiah 23:24)*

In our distress, we may not physically run away from God as Jonah tried to do, but we do run mentally. We ignore the prompting of God's Spirit and run away from His Word—as if that will ease our minds. But nothing good ever comes from ignoring God. We only find more trouble and heartache. When we sin, it not only affects us but every other life we touch.

*For innumerable evils have compassed me about: mine iniquities have taken hold upon me, so that I am not able to look up; they are more than the hairs of mine head: therefore my heart faileth me. (Psalm 40:12)*

Jonah's unfaithfulness not only caused his own trouble, but he also put at risk the innocent men in the ship that he hired to whisk him away to Tarshish. But God took Jonah's disobedience and used it as a testimony of His power to those men. They were exceedingly afraid when they learned that it was Israel's God that Jonah was fleeing from. This wasn't just any god; this was *the* God.

The ship heaved violently, the winds howled, the lashing salt spray doused the frightened men—the ship was doomed, and Jonah knew it was his fault. Yet he cared enough for these strangers, these fellow shipmates, that he agreed to be cast into the sea and die for their sake. And the men knew enough about right and wrong to be fearful of killing an innocent man and pleaded with God to not lay it to their charge. (Funny how fickle we are. One day we're running away, not caring about anyone but ourselves, another day we're willing to give ourselves up for the good of others. What a comfort to know our God never vacillates in doing what is right for us.) With Jonah overboard and the raging sea calmed, these thankful men turned to the living God, sacrificed to Him, and made vows. Sometimes our witness, however messy it is, will be the very thing God uses to convert the unbelievers in our lives.

Our manifold trials may come about through no fault of our own, or more likely, we bring them upon ourselves. In the midst of any great trial, who hasn't convinced themselves that God has left them on their own? Especially if our trial is directly related to our sinful actions, we picture an austere God who's halted His love for us, shaking His head in disappointment. We hate ourselves, we're hurting more than ever before, and we don't see any way out. But our suffering at the hand of God is not because He doesn't love us (that's just our emotions casting doubt), but because He does. "For I said in my haste, I am cut off from before thine eyes: nevertheless thou heardest the voice of my supplications when I cried unto thee" (Psalm 31:22). All is not lost and we are not forgotten. On the contrary, when we seek God, when we cry out to Him for forgiveness, no matter how far we've run, He hears us every time. "In my distress I called upon the Lord, and cried unto my God: he heard my voice out of his temple, and my cry came before him, even into his ears" (Psalm 18:6).

Jonah was in the worst way, buried alive in a fish's gut. No food, no water, putrid air to breathe, and no light whatsoever. He could have curled up and died feeling God had completely abandoned him. But he didn't. He cried out to God instead.

*When my soul fainted within me I remembered the Lord: and my prayer came in unto thee, into thine holy temple. (Jonah 2:7)*

*I will sacrifice unto thee with the voice of thanksgiving; I will pay that that I have vowed. Salvation is of the Lord. (Jonah 2:9)*

Even when things are at their worst in your life, do what Jonah did—praise God. This is your sacrifice of thanksgiving. Sacrifice your belief you deserve better. Sacrifice your bad attitude and finger-pointing. Sacrifice your desire to complain and blame and lash out and doubt. Sacrifice all these and trade them for thanksgiving, realizing how precious your salvation is. "Offer unto God thanksgiving; and pay thy vows unto the most High: And call upon me in the day of trouble: I will deliver thee, and thou shalt glorify me" (Psalm 50:14–15).

What does it mean to "pay your vows"? In the Old Testament, a vow was a free-will promise to God. A commitment to perform an act of service He then expected you to honor or "pay."

*When thou vowest a vow unto God, defer not to pay it; for he hath no pleasure in fools: pay that which thou hast vowed. (Ecclesiastes 5:4)*

When we stand at the altar, our marriage vows are a sacred promise to God and to the spouse He chose we dare not break. As Christian women, married or not, we pay our vows every day with the currency of faith, trust, and obedience to God and His Word.

*If a man vow a vow unto the Lord, or swear an oath to bind his soul with a bond; he shall not break his word, he shall do according to all that proceedeth out of his mouth. (Numbers 30:2)*

Tucked in the book of Jonah is this hidden gem: "They that observe lying vanities forsake their own mercy" (Jonah 2:8). What do we observe about ourselves, the world, or others that is not true? What falsehoods do we cling to that hamper our walk with God? To *observe lying vanities* is the same as protecting our self-interests (read: sins). We justify ourselves and guard our unsatisfactory emptiness as if it were a coveted heirloom. Do we realize what we're giving up when we choose our own ruin wrapped in a fancy package labeled "personal rights and freedom"? We forsake the mercy God wants to give us. We spend too much time defending *our* self, *our* perspective, and *our* viewpoint instead of trusting God to take care of us the way He knows best. We bury ourselves in fleshly layers of lying vanities. And in so doing, we keep back the full protection and blessings we desperately want. We are our own worst enemy. Sunk in the bowels of despair and a putrid fish, Jonah realized this truth.

## Nineveh repents and so does God

After being vomited up by the great fish, Jonah began the long walk toward his mission call. What a sight and smell he must have been to the Ninevites! The nation of Assyria had suffered much defeat since their height of power two centuries prior, and the people of Nineveh and their current king believed God would do exactly what Jonah said He would do and chose to listen to God's prophet.

The king ordered men, women, children, and even their cattle to be covered in sackcloth.[2] The king, sitting in sackcloth and ashes,[3] immediately proclaimed a fast and ordered everyone to cry out to God and turn from their evil ways. Seeing their sincerity and willingness to change, God reversed His intentions to destroy them. "And God saw their works, that they turned from their evil way; and God repented of the evil, that he had said that he would do unto them; and he did it not" (Jonah 3:10).

Yes, God repents. But His repentance is markedly different from ours. We repent by changing our minds from doing wrong, and with humble hearts, turn about and face God. With a new mindset, we begin to do what is right according to God's Word. God, in all His righteousness and mercy, changes His mind from dispensing punishment and affliction[4] once we repent and turn from our self-centered, self-righteous ways. Because God changed His mind, showing mercy to the Ninevites, Jonah sulked outside the city walls in fury. What made him stick around and not promptly return to his homeland? Was he secretly hoping to witness the destruction of the city after all? And what angered him so? Was it because the people of Nineveh did not hesistate to repent, and God thereby forgave his nation's enemy? Or was it simply because Jonah had to disrupt his life to obey God in the first place?

What angers us? As women, we go through a lot of turmoil, anguish, and pain in our lives, and sometimes it leads to anger. Anger at a God who allows us to go through fish-gut trials. We even go so far as to despair of life and wish to be done with it. But do we have a right to be angry? Are we not vessels to be used by God for our good and the good of others? "But now,

O Lord, thou art our father; we are the clay, and thou our potter; and we all are the work of thy hand" (Isaiah 64:8).

While pouting outside Nineveh's walls, Jonah cared more for the shade-giving plant God had given him that had withered overnight, than he did for all the people of Nineveh. God, through this trial of blazing heat, scorching wind, and discomfort, showed Jonah his errors in thinking. God showed him He cared for all people and was willing to save any who repented and turned to Him. No one was exempt from God's love, mercy, and redemption, not even Jonah's enemies.

## Christ and the book of Jonah side by side

The story of Nineveh's repentance parallels what Christ will do for anyone in the world. Nineveh was the enemy of Israel, but we all were, at one time, the enemies of God (Romans 5:10). Yet His love is so great toward us that He chose to die in our place. Nineveh went from hearing God's words to repentance–no running, no scoffing, no justifying themselves–and when we do the same, God sees and justifies us through Christ.

Jonah, the son of Amittai, is mentioned twice in the Bible. In the book named after him and in 2 Kings 14:25. In Matthew 10:16, we are told to be wise as serpents and harmless as doves in our Christian lives. The name *Jonah* means "dove."[5] God's Spirit descended upon Jesus Christ in the visible form of a dove after His baptism (Matthew 3:16). *Amittai* means "veracious," or, in other words, "habitually truthful, honest, trustworthy, and faithful."[6] Christ is Amittai. He is always faithful and true, and Jonah descended upon Nineveh like a dove of the Spirit offering them the only way to salvation. God gives us a part of Himself when we repent and accept Christ as our Savior—the Spirit of His Son. Wise, gentle, faithful, and true.

> *But ye are not in the flesh, but in the Spirit, if so be that the Spirit of God dwell in you. Now if any man have not the Spirit of Christ, he is none of his. (Romans 8:9)*

Jonah experienced a type of death in the depth of the sea for three days and three nights, and Christ was buried in a dark cave, the heart of the earth, for the same length of time. The Pharisees would not listen to Christ and demanded a sign that He was the Messiah, but Christ refused to give one except for the sign of the prophet Jonah. Christ also scorned the self-sufficient Pharisees by praising the men of Nineveh (unworthy gentiles to the Pharisees) who actually listened to God's Word preached to them and repented.[7]

> *For as Jonas was three days and three nights in the whale's belly; so shall the Son of man be three days and three nights in the heart of the earth.*
> *The men of Nineveh shall rise in judgment with this generation, and shall condemn it: because they repented at the preaching of Jonas; and, behold, a greater than Jonas is here. (Matthew 12:40–41)*

The book of Jonah declares that no one is exempt from God's divine love and redemption. God is no respecter of persons (Romans 10:12). We may suffer trial upon trial as Jonah did. But these trials are learning opportunities from a merciful God who wants us to stop running away out of fear and defiance, and instead, rise up in full assurance of His love and keep walking toward our mission call of faith. We may feel sadness, desolation, and yes, even anger, but God is right beside us willing to relieve our pain like a shade-giving tree in the sultry sun.

# What's the story behind . . . ?

*I went down to the bottoms of the mountains; the earth*
**with her bars** *was about me for ever. (Jonah 2:6)*

The *bars*, from this singular phrase found in the book of Jonah, are likened to the main gate of a castle, city, or stronghold shut tight between land and sea. Jonah, in the depths of the sea, in the fearful situation he found himself, envisioned heavy horizontal bolts barring him from ever getting back to land and to the living.

## Jonah notes

1. "Archaeological Supplement," in *The Original Thompson Chain-Reference Study Bible*, fourth edition (Iowa: World Bible Publishers, 1982), 351.
2. Sackcloth was a rough, uncomfortable garment made from black goat's hair worn as a symbol of grief or penitence.
3. Ashes represented desolation and ruin. Paired together with sackcloth, they were a sign of repentance and humility before God—an outward showing of what the inward man was feeling.
4. What the KJV sometimes refers to as *evil*. See also the explanation in chapter 3 under the subheading "God never does evil."
5. *Strong's* reference H3124, taken from H3123.
6. *Strong's* reference H573, taken from H571.
7. See also Matthew 16:4 and Luke 11:29–32.

6

# Micah

*Is it not for you to know judgment?*

The prophet Micah had a problem. The southern kingdom of Judah he was sent to warn expected blessings from God, but they weren't pursuing God. They were diagnosed with a terminal disease they didn't know they had. How could he get them to see this? Some Christians today are spiritually sick but don't know it. They expect to be blessed as Christians, but they don't pursue Christ. They have the Christian catchphrases down; they have the look—the Bible on their end table, the Jesus bumper stickers, and the obligatory Sunday service seat in church, but inside they are unchanged. Jesus's name is on their lips but His warnings and implorings to conform to Him sail over their self-sufficient heads. If we don't see ourselves in need of healing, like those in the prophet Micah's day, the cancer of covetousness, pride, and heartlessness grows. We cannot heal ourselves; our wound is incurable (Micah 1:9). Only God can clean our rotten flesh, our ugly spirits, and renew our lives from an inevitable and deserving death sentence. The book of Micah delivers a message of hope that promises a miraculous recovery in the form of a Savior, and the coming grace we all need to live out newly healed lives.

Micah witnessed aggressive greed and violence run rampant from the high priests to the princes to the average resident of Jerusalem. What's in it for me? How can I get even more? Take, horde, profit. They were judging wrongfully, being deceptive in trade, and worshiping idols instead of (or alongside), God. "Woe to them that devise iniquity, and work evil upon their beds! when the morning is light, they practise it, because it is in the power of their hand" (Micah 2:1). We don't want to admit that we ever think like this. Yet how often have we woken up with a self-serving agenda coursing through our minds? Thoughts of personal gain and selfish wishes? Thoughts of forcing our "rights" and hoarding forgiveness from those who've hurt us? All the while believing God is on our side.

> The heads thereof judge for reward, and the priests thereof teach for hire, and the prophets thereof divine for money: yet will they lean upon the Lord, and say, **Is not the Lord among us?** none evil can come upon us. (Micah 3:11, emphasis added)

The desire to excel in life, to want good from our relationships and gain in our bank accounts is not wrong. But when we—and the preachers of the Bible we listen to—focus solely on a me-first prosperity doctrine and omit the weightier matters of repentance, obedience, and self-sacrifice, then we foolishly believe in peace where there is none. These false teachers make mention of God but not in truth and righteousness (Isaiah 48:1). "For they have healed the hurt of the daughter of my people slightly, saying, Peace, peace; when there is no peace" (Jeremiah 8:11).

Christ is our peace. He brings us prosperity and peace of mind in a world full of takers and haters and liars. The few Bible teachers who don't merely speak "Jesus," but who defy popularity and preach personal change instead of personal gain, won't get the same fawning love (or donations). People naturally prefer words that lull them into a pillowy sense of security over words that jolt them with the truth that hey! that's a cliff of destruction you're precariously leaning over. God repeatedly sent His prophets to warn His people of that sharp drop, but most didn't want to hear about it. They didn't want to back away. "The prophets prophesy falsely, and the priests bear rule by their means; and my people love to have it so: and what will ye do in the end thereof?" (Jeremiah 5:31).

> *Prophesy ye not, say they to them that prophesy: they shall not prophesy to them, that they shall not take shame. O thou that art named the house of Jacob, **is the spirit of the Lord straitened?** are these his doings? do not my words do good to him that walketh uprightly?*
> *(Micah 2:6–7, emphasis added)*

What is the meaning of "is the spirit of the Lord straitened?" *Straitened*, in this verse, means "to cut down," or "to harvest."[1]

Did Judah's leaders think that by preventing God's prophets from speaking, they could prevent God's words, His proclamations, from reaching them? From disciplining them? From revealing their shame? God was clear that if they would only walk honestly and righteously, God promised His words would do them good.

The prophet Micah was a contemporary of the prophets Isaiah and Hosea. These men were infused with God's Spirit to proclaim His message to the same errant people at roughly the same time. Micah's years of speaking spanned the reign of Judah's three kings: Jotham, Ahaz, and Hezekiah. Father, son, and grandson respectively (Micah 1:1). But the people of Israel and Judah still reverenced the statutes of Omri and of Ahab, the despicable father and son kings of their past, and walked in their counsels, instead of the righteous counsel of Almighty God (Micah 6:16).

King Omri ruled Israel from Samaria; a mesa-like territory he purchased and named Samaria after its former owner, Shemer (1 Kings 16:24), and built altars for Baal in this newly built city with a view. Ahab, Omri's son, married the notorious Jezebel, worshipped Baal even more than his father did, and provoked God above all other kings before him. No wonder God destroyed Israel's splendor and allowed His chosen people to be enslaved yet again. They stubbornly refused to honor, worship, or put their trust in Him.

> *Woe to the rebellious children, saith the Lord, that take counsel, but not of me; and that cover with a covering, but not of my spirit, that they may add sin to sin:*
> *(Isaiah 30:1)*

*That walk to go down into Egypt, and have not asked at my mouth; to strengthen themselves in the strength of Pharaoh, and to trust in the shadow of Egypt! (Isaiah 30:2)*

## Remember Lot's wife

Like Lot's wife, the Israelites were always looking back. They glorified previous battles and victories that God had blessed, but refused to retain in their memory *why* God blessed those battles and *why* He provided them those victories. They were fond of remembering the cave of Adullum (where God protected David and his men from the evil intent of King Saul), but failed to live out the faithfulness of David, their patriarch king, whom they revered in word but not in deed. They were proud of the beauty and wealth of the many cities they secured from past God-sanctioned forays, but failed to honor God with continued reverence for those wins.

In Lachish, where the "beginning of the sin" of Israel was found,[2] Judah was trusting in the saving power of a former adversary, Egypt (the same people God helped them escape from earlier), to save them from their current adversary, Assyria, instead of trusting and hoping in their true Savior, the God of heaven. Christ warned us of this thinking: "Remember Lot's wife. Whosoever shall seek to save his life shall lose it; and whosoever shall lose his life shall preserve it" (Luke 17:32–33). Are there areas of our lives where we turn back to the perverse comforts of things God helped us escape from? To ideas and hopes and ways of living that God had already said no to for our good. God's Word will always do us good (Micah 2:7), but how often do we reach out to the wrong people and pursuits in an attempt to find rest? God's love warns us: "Arise ye, and depart; for this is not your rest: because it is polluted, it shall destroy you, even with a sore destruction" (Micah 2:10). The world cannot provide us the rest we long for. Keep in mind that each day you struggle and weep, in other words, labor, is a day closer to your true rest, God's coming kingdom.

> *There remaineth therefore a rest to the people of God. . . .*
> *Let us labour therefore to enter into that rest, lest any*
> *man fall after the same example of unbelief.*
> *(Hebrews 4:9, 11)*

When confronted by anyone who entices you to go against God's Word and the calling He's given you to live out (including your own inner voice), give them Balaam's answer to King Balak found in Numbers 22:18: "I cannot go beyond the word of the Lord my God, to do less or more."[3] We women have our orders, so to speak, which is to obey God and to pursue a faithful attitude. We cannot do less than what we know is right, nor can we add to what He's given us to do. When we follow the path God has laid for us, as narrow and rocky as it is, we will be immeasurably blessed. Blessed if we are willing to birth our bitter troubles along the way and follow the lead of God.

> *Be in pain, and labour to bring forth, O daughter of*
> *Zion, like a woman in travail: for now shalt thou go*
> *forth out of the city, and thou shalt dwell in the field, and*
> *thou shalt go even to Babylon; there shalt thou be*
> *delivered; there the Lord shall redeem thee from the hand*
> *of thine enemies. (Micah 4:10)*

Many times God leads us to places we'd rather not go. Over a hundred years after the ten tribes that made up the northern kingdom of Israel were conquered and completely dispersed by the Assyrian Empire, God told the conquered southern kingdom of Judah that in order to be saved they needed to be led by their captors to Babylon. They knew what had happened to their brother nation, but they were told to trust God. We have to enter our Babylon too. Where galling trials and soul-stretching growth occur. We have to be willing to leave the comfort of our false thinking and trust God to lead us where He will. Doing so feels like labor pangs, but only in our surrender to God will we find deliverance from a multitude of fears and doubts that confine us. We emerge stronger in faith when we allow God to take us away from where we started. We live mighty in spirit and power to conquer our enemies (Micah 5:9)—the physical, spiritual, and mental enemies that hold us down and shackle us to joylessness, ungratefulness, and meanness of spirit.

## The Lord's controversy
Even with all God had done for Israel and Judah, they still turned away. The pull of the world they lived in was stronger than their love and gratitude for Him.

> *Hear ye, O mountains, the Lord's controversy, and ye strong foundations of the earth: for the Lord hath a controversy with his people, and he will plead with Israel.*
> *O my people, what have I done unto thee? and wherein have I wearied thee? testify against me. (Micah 6:2–3)*

Like ancient Israel, we are not exempt from this pull. We must resist the world's glittering deceptions dangling in our faces each day and not be offended by what God requires us to do. "For this is the love of God, that we keep his commandments: and his commandments are not grievous" (1 John 5:3). These commandments are found in Micah. "He hath shewed thee, O man, what is good; and what doth the Lord require of thee, but to do justly, and to love mercy, and to walk humbly with thy God?" (Micah 6:8). Micah knew it wasn't the rituals, the rote obedience, or living by "letter of the law" that would pleased God, but simply to:

1. Do the right thing.
2. Love one another (inconvenient and irksome as it may be).
3. Live quietly content and respectful toward God.

But these three edicts require an earnest heart-change of self-sacrifice, patience, trust, long-suffering, forgiveness, and accepting the answer of no to our manifold dreams. A life of self-denial is impossible if we don't look beyond this life and keep our focus on our Savior, Jesus Christ. When we do, look what God has promised His faithful in the book of Micah. What undeserved grace God showers us with! He pardons our sins because He delights in mercy.

*Who is a God like unto thee, that pardoneth iniquity, and passeth by the transgression of the remnant of his heritage? he retaineth not his anger for ever, because he delighteth in mercy. (Micah 7:18)*

*He will turn again, he will have compassion upon us; he*
*will subdue our iniquities; and thou wilt cast all their*
*sins into the depths of the sea. (Micah 7:19)*

"Who is a God like unto thee?" said Micah. Interestingly
enough, the name *Micah* means "who is like Jah?"[4] *Jah* translates
to "the Lord."[5] Micah witnessed perverted justice, bribery, hatred,
and mischief of all kinds. He was so distraught that he believed, as
Elijah did in his cave,[6] that there were no godly people left in the
land (Micah 7:1–4). He felt alone and despondent and could not
even confide his distress to his own wife. "Trust ye not in a friend,
put ye not confidence in a guide: keep the doors of thy mouth
from her that lieth in thy bosom" (Micah 7:5). Micah refers to his
enemy in verse 10 as "she" instead of the more common pronoun
"he." How sad it must have been for Micah to not be able to trust
his own mate, to come home to contention and grief.

*For the son dishonoureth the father, the daughter riseth*
*up against her mother, the daughter in law against her*
*mother in law; a man's enemies are the men of his own*
*house. (Micah 7:6)*

A family not spiritually united but adversarial instead is a
heart-rending reality for some. Christ expounded upon Micah's
words when He told his disciples in Matthew 10:35–36 that
obedience to Him would be the catalyst for family division in
the Christian's life. "For I am come to set a man at variance
against his father, and the daughter against her mother, and the
daughter in law against her mother in law. And a man's foes
shall be they of his own household."

Many husbands and wives blame the other for the reason they lash out in anger. In their pain, they feel justified in withholding forgiveness. A perpetual cycle of resentment gets started they don't know how to stop. But Micah understood his personal responsibility to own up to his sins and not blame those around him. He knew being humble before God was the only path to peace. Micah trusted God to judge righteously.

> *I will bear the indignation of the Lord, because I have sinned against him, until he plead my cause, and execute judgment for me: he will bring me forth to the light, and I shall behold his righteousness. (Micah 7:9)*

When we admit our sins, God lifts us up. He brings us to His light so we can see His mercy firsthand. But when a man and his wife refuse to admit their sins to God and to each other, when the two do not live as one god-fearing unit, there is no peace. Divisions, arguments, and mayhem abound.

> *Then she that is mine enemy shall see it, and shame shall cover her which said unto me, Where is the Lord thy God? mine eyes shall behold her: now shall she be trodden down as the mire of the streets. (Micah 7:10)*

How troubling when a spouse taunts the other's faith in God, as Micah, David, and Job intimately understood. But even in harmonious marriages, there are times when either one might mock the other, or refuse to listen, causing the grip of loneliness to tighten around their spouse's heart. No one is loving at all times. God knew this and calls us to remember

Micah's words: "Therefore I will look unto the Lord; I will wait for the God of my salvation: my God will hear me" (Micah 7:7).

## Christ's earthly beginning and heavenly kingdom

The book of Micah has the distinguished honor of being the only Old Testament book to proclaim the town of Bethlehem as the birthplace of Christ. The Gospel of Matthew makes reference to this passage.

> *But thou, Beth–lehem Ephratah, though thou be little among the thousands of Judah, yet out of thee shall he come forth unto me that is to be ruler in Israel; whose goings forth have been from of old, from everlasting.* (Micah 5:2)

> *And thou Bethlehem, in the land of Juda, art not the least among the princes of Juda: for out of thee shall come a Governor, that shall rule my people Israel.* (Matthew 2:6)

The opening of Micah chapter 4 paints a delightful picture of the beginning of the millennium. You will find the prophet Isaiah used nearly identical wording in Isaiah 2:2–4. (Being contemporaries, did they compare notes?)

> *And many nations shall come, and say, Come, and let us go up to the mountain of the Lord, and to the house of the God of Jacob; and he will teach us of his ways, and we will walk in his paths: for the law shall go forth of Zion, and the word of the Lord from Jerusalem.* (Micah 4:2)

*And he shall judge among many people, and rebuke strong nations afar off; and they shall beat their swords into plowshares, and their spears into pruninghooks: nation shall not lift up a sword against nation, neither shall they learn war any more. (Micah 4:3)*

At the end of the tribulation described in Revelation chapters 19 through 21, Christ descends with a shout and the trump of God (1 Thessalonians 4:16) to usher in His thousand-year reign as King of Kings and Lord of Lords. "In that day," Christ will thoroughly destroy all witchcraft, falsehood, iniquity, everything contrary to Him and will "execute vengeance in anger and fury upon the heathen, such as they have not heard" (Micah 5:15). Not every word of prophecy is immediately understood, but Micah chapter 4 suggests that people still living after the tribulation who did not worship the beast (Revelation 13) or get its mark (Revelation 16:2) will begin to learn a new way to live their lives. They will stop living in hatred and violence and start living in the love and mercy of He who is Faithful and True (Revelation 19:11). God says they will learn war no more, but "beat their swords into plowshares, and spears into pruning hooks" (Micah 4:3; Isaiah 2:4), the reverse of what He told the rebellious to do in the valley of decision in Joel chapter 3.

Here is a curious thought: Micah 4:5 says "For all people will walk every one in the name of his god, and we will walk in the name of the Lord our God for ever and ever" (Micah 4:5). Is this reference to god (lowercase g) referring to us? In the millennium, those of us who follow and obey God now, who are His children of light now, will be transformed into spirit beings like unto Him (1 Corinthians 15:51–52). But some of our uncalled friends and family—the "nations" as implied by Micah chapter 4—will enter the millennium as physical human beings or be resurrected shortly after the millennium (see Joel notes 4), and will need to be taught the ways of the Lord. We will be their "gods," so to speak. We will be kings and priests of God (Revelation 5:10) guiding and teaching them of the righteousness of God. What exciting times it will be!

These parting words in the book of Micah should comfort us all: "Thou wilt perform the truth to Jacob, and the mercy to Abraham, which thou hast sworn unto our fathers from the days of old" (Micah 7:20). We are inundated with deception and unmerciful acts every day, things Micah witnessed firsthand. But he knew God's justice would prevail. He knew truth and mercy, God's consummated love, would engulf the world leaving nothing else. We, as women who trust in the promises of God, can rest in that knowledge too.

## What's the story behind...?

*Make thee bald, and **poll thee for thy delicate children;** enlarge thy baldness as the eagle; for they are gone into captivity from thee. (Micah 1:16)*

As a sign of remorse and humility during mourning, it was customary for the men of Israel (and for many Gentile nations) to shave their heads. To *poll* is another word for shaving, shearing, or cutting off. *Delicate* in this verse means "delightful or pleasant." Israel was instructed to mourn for the loss of their home, their city, and their children who would never go back to their homeland, but instead would die in captivity.

# Micah notes

1. *Strong's* reference H7114.
2. Lachish was the first of the cities of Judah that gave in to the idolatry of Jeroboam. "Micah 1:13 commentary" from *John Gill's Exposition of the Bible*, Bible Study Tools, accessed April 23, 2025, https://www.biblestudytools.com/commentaries/gills-exposition-of-the-bible/micah-1-13.html#g.
3. See also Micah 6:5.
4. *Strong's* reference H4321, taken from H4320; which is a combination of H4310 and H3050.
5. *Strong's* reference H3050: taken from H3068; *YHWH*, the *self-Existent* or *Eternal*; *Jehovah*, the Jewish national name of God.
6. See 1 Kings 19:14–18.

# Nahum

*Who can stand before His indignation?*

Not much is known about the prophet Nahum. He's only mentioned once in all the Bible, but God chose Nahum to proclaim the destruction of Nineveh. Yes, the same Nineveh God spared a hundred years before when He sent Jonah to warn them their time was short, and they had better repent. Nineveh, the capital of the Assyrian empire, had turned back to rebellion, violence, and witchcraft, and God had had enough.

Nineveh brutally devoured the cities round about them like voracious worms on a food-producing field. But Nahum declared as "the cankerworm spoileth and flieth away . . . and their place is not known where they are," so would Nineveh's strength and grandeur (Nahum 3:16–17). God is exceedingly patient with all people, but there comes a time when He says "enough" (Revelation 22:11). And Nahum's job was to shout enough! to wicked, ruthless Nineveh.

The prophet Nahum, whose name means *consolation*,[1] consoles us with a sampling of the multitude of God's virtues in the first chapter of this three-chapter book.

- God is jealous for you (1:2).
- God is slow to anger (1:3).
- God is all-powerful (1:3–5).
- God is good (1:7).
- God knows who are His (1:7).
- God will destroy our enemies (1:8–10).

Did you know God is jealous for you? We often think of jealousy as a sinful emotional reaction, yet one of God's many wondrous names is Jealous. "For thou shalt worship no other god: for the Lord, whose name is Jealous, is a jealous God" (Exodus 34:14).

> *God is jealous, and the Lord revengeth; the Lord revengeth, and is furious; the Lord will take vengeance on his adversaries, and he reserveth wrath for his enemies. (Nahum 1:2)*

You are God's treasure and called by His holy name, and He will fight off legions of evil for your sake. When you suffer injustice, He will not forget. Those who caused you wrongful pain will be held accountable. That's how jealous God is for you.

In a marriage, if there is a hint of infidelity, husbands (and wives) become rightfully jealous and resentfully suspicious of a rival. And if a husband finds out his wife was, in fact, unfaithful to him, it crushes him and drives him to fury—against the woman who hurt him and against the one she chose to love more than him. This is how ancient Israel treated her Husband, the Almighty. Other nations and their gods were more important to her. But marriage calls for exclusive loyalty to a spouse. God was jealous for Israel and He is jealous for us and will not allow anyone or anything to intrude upon our union with Him. The Israelites provoked God to jealousy often, and sadly, many of us do the same when we allow the furrows we plow in this world to bury our first love (Revelation 2:4).

> *Ye cannot drink the cup of the Lord, and the cup of devils: ye cannot be partakers of the Lord's table, and of the table of devils.*
> *Do we provoke the Lord to jealousy? are we stronger than he? (1 Corinthians 10:21–22)*

Jealousy is a part of being human. If your best friend spends more time with another friend than she does with you, you might feel jealousy. If your husband behaves extra friendly toward another woman, even if it's completely innocent, you're almost guaranteed to feel jealousy. If someone else receives the very thing you've longed for, prayed for, and cried over, jealousy creeps up brazen—oh, why couldn't I have gotten that?—and defiles you with self-pity if you're not careful. King Saul was awash in jealousy and self-pity when young David garnered more acclaim from battle than he had, and in 1 Samuel 18:8 he said, "They have ascribed unto David ten thousands, and to me they have ascribed but thousands: and what can he have more but the kingdom?" You can almost hear the whine in his voice. Don't confuse jealousy with envy. When you feel envy, you resent and harbor ill will toward the person who has the advantages and possessions you want but don't have, like Saul eventually felt toward David. There is no such thing as godly envy, but there is godly jealousy.

> For I am jealous over you with godly jealousy: for I have espoused you to one husband, that I may present you as a chaste virgin to Christ. (2 Corinthians 11:2)

Jealousy can make us fiercely protective of our loved one's heart and their affections toward us, which is an honorable reaction. But jealousy can also cause us to feel sorry for ourselves or drive us to envy. Only God's jealousy is pure. God's name is holy and with godly jealousy He guards His name's sake. He doesn't want us polluting His name by claiming we are His but living like harlots instead (1 Corinthians 6:15). God knows our best place is by His side. He knows our most content lives are lived within His generous and loving boundaries. He gives us free will to accept or deny our calling. But if we deny God's goodness, if we refuse His will, what do we have to look forward to but a life of doubts and sorrows, scrabbling and clamor, and eventually, the finality of His coming wrath (Hebrews 3:12)?

God is always good, but as we do the hard work of trusting Him, His goodness flows freely into our lives and our natural fear of losing our hopes, our dreams, our very selves, recedes. What comfort Nahum spoke: "The Lord is good, a stronghold in the day of trouble; and he knoweth them that trust in him" (Nahum 1:7).

## No place for repentance

The inhabitants of Nineveh came to a point of no return. They provoked God by refusing the mercy and goodness He lovingly gave them a century before. They preferred living by wicked pursuits and prevailed in them with an air of superiority. Like young lions, Nineveh didn't fear anyone (Nahum 2:11–12). But "who can stand before [God's] indignation? and who can abide in the fierceness of his anger?" (Nahum 1:6). Every day the wicked, godless haters of this world are committing horrendous crimes and slipping out of justice's grip, but God has not forgotten, His grip is iron and "will not at all acquit the wicked" (Nahum 1:3).

*And the Lord hath given a commandment concerning thee, that no more of thy name be sown. (Nahum 1:14)*

*Behold, I am against thee, saith the Lord of hosts, and I will burn her chariots in the smoke, and the sword shall devour thy young lions: and I will cut off thy prey from the earth, and the voice of thy messengers shall no more be heard. (Nahum 2:13)*

God promised to make a final end of Nineveh and in the year 612 BC, the last year of Nahum's prophecy, Nineveh was indeed destroyed. Its ruins were so deeply buried they were not identified until AD 1845.[2] Christ promises at His righteous return to make an utter end to anyone, whole nations down to the single individual, who revels in evil as Nineveh did. The prophecies spoken by Nahum overlapped the prophecies spoken by Jeremiah. By the time Jeremiah prophesied, the destruction of Assyria, with Nineveh its capital, had already happened.

*Therefore thus saith the Lord of hosts, the God of Israel;*
*Behold, I will punish the king of Babylon and his land,*
*as I have punished the king of Assyria. (Jeremiah 50:18)*

Assyria was a savage kingdom filled with atrocities and cruelty, but its final end was secured by the might of God's righteous judgment. "All that hear the bruit of thee shall clap their hands over thee: for upon whom hath not thy wickedness passed continually?" (Nahum 3:19). The word *bruit* in the King James Version means "announcement, something heard, news, or report."[3] When the outlying cities were to hear of Nineveh's demise, they would be thoroughly glad (clapping their hands) for all the terror and destruction previously inflicted upon them by Nineveh. Not only was Nineveh cruel, but sure of its power and filled with pride and arrogance.

*Art thou better than populous No, that was situate*
*among the rivers, that had the waters round about it,*
*whose rampart was the sea, and her wall was from the*
*sea? . . .*
*Yet was she carried away . . . and all her great men were*
*bound in chains. (Nahum 3:8, 10)*

"Populous No," also known as Thebes, was sacked by Assyria in 663 BC, the beginning of Nahum's prophecy. Fifty years later, Assyria, along with Nineveh, its capital, was sacked by Babylon. God used Assyria to take down the city of No and used Babylon to take down Assyria. (God later punished Babylon for its wickedness too.) Nineveh could not save herself. No one who fights against God can. Nineveh's strength was likened to overripe figs dropped into the waiting mouth of the eater God brought to destroy her (Nahum 3:12).

> *Behold, I am against thee, saith the Lord of hosts; and I*
> *will discover thy skirts upon thy face, and I will shew the*
> *nations thy nakedness, and the kingdoms thy shame.*
> *And I will cast abominable filth upon thee, and make*
> *thee vile, and will set thee as a gazingstock.*
> *(Nahum 3:5–6)*

Nineveh thought she was lovely; God thought she was vile (Nahum 1:14). She could not justify her strength, her wealth, or her importance in the world to Him. Neither can we. We cannot stand before God and prove anything except how vile we are apart from Him. When the Bible speaks of abominable filth, no matter who we are or where we come from, we can all agree on the definition. It's something none of us wants to be covered in. Yet, this is what God says will happen to those who live by pride and evil (Nahum 3:6).

Many unfavorable descriptions of Nineveh found in the book of Nahum parallel the descriptions of ancient Israel found throughout the Bible.

| | |
|---|---|
| 1) Nahum cried against Nineveh, "Woe to the bloody city! it is all full of lies and robbery; the prey departeth not" (Nahum 3:1). | Jerusalem was also a bloody city that stored up robbery and violence in her palaces (Amos 3:10; Ezekiel 24:9). |

| | |
|---|---|
| 2) Nineveh behaved as a well-favored harlot (Nahum 3:4). | But according to God, Israel and Judah did shamefully worse (Jeremiah 3:6–11, 20; Ezekiel 16:15). |
| 3) Nahum cried against Nineveh again, "There is no healing of thy bruise; thy wound is grievous" (Nahum 3:19). | Jerusalem's wound was grievous and incurable too because they refused to believe they needed healing (Micah 1:9). |
| 4) Nineveh sold nations through her whoredoms and families through her witchcraft (Nahum 3:4). | Many wicked kings of Israel and Judah did likewise (2 Chronicles 33:6). |

The priests of Israel sold whole families into error by ignoring God's commands and making excuses for disobedience. The same satanic spirit that infected Nineveh and Babylon, and all the nations of the world since, is the same spirit that will fight against God's chosen people (us) in the tribulation as recorded in Revelation 17:5–6.

God turned away the excellency (meaning *pride* or *arrogancy* in the KJV[4]) of Jacob by means of captivity and famine and hardships to draw them closer to Him (Nahum 2:2; Amos 6:8). Some humbled themselves and turned back to God. Some didn't. God turns away our excellency, our reliance on ourselves and anything and everything we hold up higher than Him, for our own good as well. What we can learn from the book of Nahum and the downfall of Nineveh is this: (1) never trust in money, status, or strength to get us through this life, (2) never believe we are not exempt from correction, (3) never take God's gift of mercy for granted, and (4) after we repent, never, ever go back to the filth of the world in which we have escaped (2 Peter 2:20–22).

## Our beautiful feet

*How beautiful upon the mountains are the feet of him that bringeth good tidings, that publisheth peace; that bringeth good tidings of good, that publisheth salvation; that saith unto Zion, Thy God reigneth! (Isaiah 52:7)*

Nahum repeated the prophet Isaiah's words about the beauty of those who bravely declare the good news of peace that only comes through our Savior.

*Behold upon the mountains the feet of him that bringeth good tidings, that publisheth peace! (Nahum 1:15)*

And Paul reminded us from the book of Nahum this same truth in Romans:

*And how shall they preach, except they be sent? as it is written, How beautiful are the feet of them that preach the gospel of peace, and bring glad tidings of good things! (Romans 10:15)*

We may be physically challenged, financially poor, not accomplished or attractive at all by the world's standards, but none of these "deficiencies" matter to God. We are beautiful to Him when we show others the righteousness, mercy, and peace of God through our daily, faithful living.

# What's the story behind…?

*And **Huzzab** shall be led away captive, she shall be brought up, and her maids shall lead her as with the voice of doves, tabering upon their breasts. (Nahum 2:7)*

No other Bible translation except the KJV uses the word *Huzzab*. This word (of unknown origin) means to *station*, to be *appointed, set over, stand upright*.[5] A mistake in translation, Huzzab was not intended to be a capitalized place name, but as a metaphor for something solid like a pillar, an immovable state, an appointed position (like a king or queen) that ends up, in the verse above, not being as established as they thought and easily taken down.

# Nahum notes

1. *Strong's* reference H5151, taken from H5162.
2. "Archaeological Supplement," in *The Original Thompson Chain-Reference Study Bible*, fourth edition (Iowa: World Bible Publishers, 1982), 351.
3. *Strong's* reference H8088.
4. *Strong's* reference H1346 and H1347.
5. *Strong's* reference H5324.

# *Habakkuk*

*Yet I will rejoice in the Lord*

Who hasn't grappled with understanding God's Word or trusting in His judgment? Who hasn't felt despair in the midst of their trials or wondered where God was in their pain? As Christians, we all have, and Habakkuk was no different. Habakkuk's name means *embrace*.[1] But this embracing was less like gentle hugging and more like clasping or grappling. Habakkuk grappled with the agonizing truth that God would destroy Jerusalem by sending a terrifying enemy to bring her down. But Habakkuk also clung tightly to the mercy of God, and so can we. "O Lord, I have heard thy speech, and was afraid: O Lord, revive thy work in the midst of the years, in the midst of the years make known; in wrath remember mercy" (Habakkuk 3:2).

In our tragic circumstances, like a miscarriage, a cancer diagnosis, a house fire, or the loss of family income, it's common to cry out, "Where are you, God?" And when wicked men get away with evil and the godly suffer because of it, we wonder why, as Habakkuk did.

*Thou art of purer eyes than to behold evil, and canst not look on iniquity: wherefore lookest thou upon them that deal treacherously, and holdest thy tongue when the wicked devoureth the man that is more righteous than he? (Habakkuk 1:13)*

In his frustration, Habakkuk posed the thought that maybe God chose not to see the evil or intervene because He was too pure to look upon it. Habakkuk knew God could wipe out Judah's enemies in an instant, but in his anguish, he posed the internal question, *Is that why the wicked prosper?*

More than a century before Habakkuk was written, in 722 BC, God sent the Assyrians to conquer the northern kingdoms of Israel and Samaria as punishment for their widespread disobedience, idol worship, and greed. And yet the southern kingdom of Judah hadn't learned anything from their brother's captivity during the succeeding 130 years. They continued down the same path of wickedness and violence and God raised the Babylonians, "that bitter and hasty nation," against them (Habakkuk 1:6).

God sent the Babylonians to humble Judah, but Babylon would not be drunk on her glory forever. The cup of the Lord's right hand would spew shame upon them (Habakkuk 2:16). Like the Assyrians before them, God procured Babylon's doom

for their insatiable covetousness and violence. What they meted
out would come back upon them (Habakkuk 2:5, 8).

The Babylonians (called *Chaldeans* in the KJV) were a fear-
some nation. They conquered the powerful Assyrian and Egyptian
empires, both of which had previously enslaved the Israelites,
and believed there was nothing or no one that could master
them. They were a law unto themselves (Habakkuk 1:7–10). As
a prophet of God knowing ahead of time that his nation would be
annihilated and his people destroyed brought Habakkuk great
sorrow and understandable feelings of despair. He cried out to
God as King David and King Asaph recorded in the Psalms had
numerous times before.

> *My God, my God, why hast thou forsaken me? why art
> thou so far from helping me, and from the words of my
> roaring?*
> *O my God, I cry in the daytime, but thou hearest not; and
> in the night season, and am not silent. (Psalm 22:1–2)*

> *Will the Lord cast off for ever? and will he be favourable
> no more?*
> *Is his mercy clean gone for ever? doth his promise fail for
> evermore?*
> *Hath God forgotten to be gracious? hath he in anger shut
> up his tender mercies? Selah. (Psalm 77:7–9)*

But Habakkuk knew *why* the enemy was coming. He
watched his people revel in sinfulness his whole life and it
grieved him. "Therefore the law is slacked, and judgment doth
never go forth: for the wicked doth compass about the righteous;

therefore wrong judgment proceedeth" (Habakkuk 1:4). The prophet Habakkuk understood God was sending the Babylonians for Judah's judgment and correction. He also knew God wouldn't destroy His people entirely. He had hope in the long-term promises of God and comforted himself with the belief that "we shall not die."

> *Art thou not from everlasting, O Lord my God, mine Holy One? we shall not die. O Lord, thou hast ordained them for judgment; and, O mighty God, thou hast established them for correction. (Habakkuk 1:12)*

We are God's beloved daughters, and He corrects everyone He loves. Correction is exceedingly painful while we're going through it. Spiritual pruning hurts, but won't kill us. On the contrary, what we learn from and repent of because of God-touched correction brings with it everlasting life.

> *Blessed be the Lord, who daily loadeth us with benefits, even the God of our salvation. Selah.*
> *He that is our God is the God of salvation; and unto God the Lord belong the issues from death.*
> *(Psalm 68:19–20)*

God alone is our escape from death. Disease and aging as we know it did not exist in the Garden of Eden but came after man chose to be his own god. On one extreme, people try to escape death by putting their faith in doctors, medicines, or surgeries. And on the other, by putting their faith in nutritional supplements and a healthy lifestyle. But eventually, everyone dies. Although Habakkuk's words, "we shall not die," referred to protection from national extinction, it is comforting to know as we age and draw closer to physical death that God protects us from spiritual extinction with promises of eternal life through faith in Christ.

## Paul quotes Habakkuk twice

Self-righteousness, an attitude we may not realize we harbor, is what condemns us. We think we are good, but we're not (Romans 1:10; Psalm 53:1–3).

> *Behold, his soul which is lifted up is not upright in him: but the just shall live by his faith. (Habakkuk 2:4)*

> *For therein is the righteousness of God revealed from faith to faith: as it is written, The just shall live by faith. (Romans 1:17)*

> *But that no man is justified by the law in the sight of God, it is evident: for, The just shall live by faith. (Galatians 3:11)*

Paul made clear the impossibility of being justified by the Mosaic Law throughout his letters to the churches. It is only through our faith in God and His Son, Jesus Christ, that we are justified. When you are faithful, you are just. You are just (righteous, innocent, and holy) only because you abide in Christ by faith. God makes provision for us through His Word. He teaches, warns, comforts, and prepares us throughout the Bible (especially in the letters of Paul, Peter, and James) for how to live and what His faithful children can expect for the future—a glorious eternity of peace and love.

The people of Israel and Judah were repeatedly warned to change their ways and return to God (or else), but they refused to believe the dire proclamations of the prophets God sent. Habakkuk declared to the men of Judah, "I will work a work in your days, which ye will not believe, though it be told you" (Habakkuk 1:5). Paul, preaching at Antioch, quoted this same passage from Habakkuk to the disbelieving Jews about Christ. "Behold, ye despisers, and wonder, and perish: for I work a work in your days, a work which ye shall in no wise believe, though a man declare it unto you" (Acts 13:41).

The majority of the Jews Paul spoke to refused to believe the good news of the Messiah, but the Gentiles did not refuse. No matter what the Jews had seen or heard concerning Jesus Christ—His miracles and words of undeniable truth and power—many stubbornly refused to believe. They hardened their hearts. Long before Paul stood preaching, the tribe of Judah sought idols over the law of Moses and now the Pharisees, in Paul's day, sought the law of Moses to justify them and to be their god.

Idolatry has been around forever. The prideful Babylonians gave credit for their power to their gods (Habakkuk 1:11) and Israel and Judah often trusted in their "teacher of lies" more than the Most High.

*What profiteth the graven image that the maker thereof hath graven it; the molten image, and a teacher of lies, that the maker of his work trusteth therein, to make dumb idols? (Habakkuk 2:18)*

*Woe unto him that saith to the wood, Awake; to the dumb stone, Arise, it shall teach! Behold ... there is no breath at all in the midst of it. (Habakkuk 2:19)*

In our modern days, we read about this practice of idol worship in our Bibles and shake our heads thinking how could they be so foolish? It's just a hunk of rock or a chunk of wood. But what do we hold in our hands, in our hearts, that has the same potential to steer us away from God and replace His glory?

- Anything we run to in our pain other than God is an idol.
- Anything we expect to fulfill us more than God is an idol.
- Any aspiration we serve more than God is an idol.
- Anyone we love more than God is an idol.

We really are no different from the Israelites. We have made idols out of things that have no hope or love or power in them. Yes, God gave us women desires to pursue and people to love and things that make us happy—all good gifts to enjoy—but none of these things takes precedence over the Giver Himself. God doesn't want us enslaved by the world, laboring in vain for things that can't give life. Only the knowledge of God can do that. The world loves to suppress the knowledge of God, but someday nothing but that will remain (Habakkuk 2:14; Isaiah 11:9).

While Habakkuk grappled with the burden of what God told him would befall Jerusalem, God told him to be patient and believe. "For the vision is yet for an appointed time, but at the end it shall speak, and not lie: though it tarry, wait for it; because it will surely come, it will not tarry" (Habakkuk 2:3). And two years later it did. What God said would happen, happened. With patience and faith, we can trust in the promise of Christ's return, for this gives our life hope and meaning. In Hebrews 10:36–38, we are told our waiting for "yet a little while" in faith will not be in vain.

## The song of Habakkuk

In this third and final chapter, after Habakkuk waxes eloquent on the brightness and power of God, he makes a profound statement:

> *Although the fig tree shall not blossom, neither shall fruit be in the vines; the labour of the olive shall fail, and the fields shall yield no meat; the flock shall be cut off from the fold, and there shall be no herd in the stalls: Yet I will rejoice in the Lord, I will joy in the God of my salvation. (Habakkuk 3:17–18)*

As Christian women we must ask ourselves: if everything that brings us happiness disappeared tomorrow, would we still praise God? Habakkuk understood loss and within these two verses provided the only remedy for the grief that befalls us all.

- Are you living with devastating losses and dead dreams? Praise God anyway.
- Has the herd of prosperity left your stalls, and are you feeling alone and cut off from the fold? Praise God anyway.

- Has your body failed you like a blossomless tree, and has the vine of your hopes withered? Praise God anyway.
- Has your hard work yielded nothing but sorrow, and has the field of promise you sowed lain fallow? Praise God anyway.

Praising God is how you keep going without despair consuming you whole. Being grateful for each blessing—your very breath is a blessing—keeps you strong. You may see nothing that looks like a blessing right now, but that nothing cannot be compared to the everything waiting for you in the kingdom of God. Look beyond the pain and disappointment of this life, and the dreams that didn't come true, and keep your eyes on the greatest of all dreams come true: eternal life. Joy is possible in the hardship and the ugliness of life when you focus on the undeserved gift of salvation God has lovingly saved for you.

"Although the fig tree shall not blossom . . ." Especially now when everything is amiss in our lives, we need to praise God and rest in Him. As Habakkuk sought rest in his day of trouble (Habakkuk 3:16), so can we. We hear frightening news every day. Those in charge push fear to control the world they worship. This world is their god, and they will fight for its continuance by their humanistic governance, spewing predictions of doom with climate change, gun control, racial division, or a worldwide pandemic to control the masses. But we know God's prophecies are the truth. We have no reason to fear when we put our trust in God.

Habakkuk quoted King David[2] when he wrote: "The Lord God is my strength, and he will make my feet like hinds' feet, and he will make me to walk upon mine high places"

(Habakkuk 3:19). Our strength does not stem from our good health, our bank accounts, or our positions of prestige. These temporary things could disappear overnight. It is God who strengthens us spiritually so we can walk with confidence in our trials, not stumble, but stand firm in His promises. *Hinds* (as deer were called in the KJV) walked treacherous, rocky paths with confidence. God's Spirit gives us mental and emotional stability to navigate our rough and chaotic world. Our *high places* are where we worship God, in congregations large and small, quiet moments on the back porch, sleepy in our beds at night, or in the bustle of keeping house and raising children.

God makes it possible for us to worship Him even in the midst of disaster and deprivation. In difficult times, we tend to seek temporary fixes—social media, food, alcohol, entertainment—to soothe our frayed nerves and troubled minds. But God has much more to give us if we seek Him first and foremost. The whole of Psalm 13 sums up the mighty struggle Habakkuk faced. Like him, we might start out grappling with doubts of God's love as shown in verses 1 through 4:

> *How long wilt thou forget me, O Lord? for ever? how long wilt thou hide thy face from me?*
> *How long shall I take counsel in my soul, having sorrow in my heart daily? how long shall mine enemy be exalted over me?*
> *Consider and hear me, O Lord my God: lighten mine eyes, lest I sleep the sleep of death;*
> *Lest mine enemy say, I have prevailed against him; and those that trouble me rejoice when I am moved.*
> *(Psalm 13:1–4)*

But if we proclaim the truth of God's mercy and salvation as Habakkuk did, we will end up at peace praising His name with a resolute melody on our lips:

*But I have trusted in thy mercy; my heart shall rejoice in thy salvation.*
*I will sing unto the Lord, because he hath dealt bountifully with me. (Psalm 13:5–6)*

# What's the story behind...?

*God came from **Teman**, and the Holy One from mount*
***Paran**. (Habakkuk 3:3)*

The book of Habakkuk, much like the other eleven books of
the Minor Prophets, is filled with obscure poetic passages. What
did Habakkuk mean by "God came from Teman, and the Holy
One from mount Paran" (Habakkuk 3:3)?

*Teman* means "from the south"[3] and is a reference to the
Sinai desert the Israelites traveled through after God rescued
them from slavery in Egypt. Mount Paran, also known as
Mount Sinai,[4] was the place God gave them the law. God then
lead them north past Mount Paran toward the promised land.
Jesus Christ is our promised land. *Paran* means "to gleam,
embellish, beautify, and to make clear."[5] The Israelites started
with the law of God (the Old Testament) until the bright and
shining hope of His Son, Jesus Christ (the New Testament)
appeared that gives us freedom from death and shame and clears
the way for eternal life with Him.

# Habakkuk notes

1. *Strong's* reference H2265.
2. See 2 Samuel 22:34 and Psalm 18:33.
3. *Strong's* reference H8487.
4. Bryant G. Wood, PhD, "What Do Mt. Horeb, The Mountain Of God, Mt. Paran And Mt. Seir Have To Do With Mt. Sinai?," Associates for Biblical Research, November 17, 2008, accessed April 23, 2025, https://biblearchaeology.org/research/chronological-categories/exodus-era/4012-what-do-mt-horeb-the-mountain-of-god-mt-paran-and-mt-seir-have-to-do-with-mt-sinai.
5. *Strong's* reference H6290, taken from H6286.

9

# Zephaniah

*Hold thy peace at the presence of the Lord*

God's love for us is astounding. We were filthy, yet He made us clean (John 15:3). We were lost, yet He searched long to find us (Ezekiel 34:16). We were dead because of sin, yet God graciously gave us life through the sacrifice of His Son, Jesus Christ. In the book of Zephaniah, God pleads with us to seek Him, to obey Him, and to live righteously and humbly so we might be hidden in the day of the Lord (Zephaniah 2:3). Zephaniah's name means "Jah [the Lord] has secreted."[1] *Secreted* means, "to hide, to reserve, to protect, and to deny." God wants to hide us under His wing, to reserve us unto Himself, to protect us from evil, and to deny us His coming wrath. How wonderful to be secreted by God! And because He will do this, what better reason is there for why we are told to sing in Zephaniah 3:14?

Entrance into God's coming kingdom means He has reversed our rightful judgment. He has cast out our enemy. All the sins of our past, all the things we wish we could reverse, He will. God will gather all our sorrows and remove them from existence. Trials that plagued us and regrets that smothered our peace will vaporize in a twinkling of an eye. We won't be able to stop the exultant shout of gladness radiating from our newly-formed throats.

Most prophecies in the Minor Prophets have a dual purpose. First, they warned the original recipients of God's soon-to-be-wielded judgment, and secondly, they warn the modern world of future judgment. The book of Zephaniah opens with dire proclamations against Jerusalem for their rebellion, and against Moab and Ammon[2] for their pride and wickedness, but it also foreshadows events of the end times that apply to us all.

The books of the Bible do not always sit in precise chronological order. That is the case for Zephaniah. The book of Zephaniah comes after the book of Nahum in our Bibles, yet Zephaniah's ministry fell in the middle of Nahum's ministry that prophesied and witnessed the final end of Nineveh. So, while God pronounced the destruction of Moab and Ammon and several other kingdoms that were hostile to Jerusalem (including Assyria and her capital, Nineveh) in the second chapter of the book of Zephaniah, Nineveh had yet to be destroyed.

Zephaniah spoke of the wealth and power of Moab, Ammon, Assyria, and the four cities of Canaan that were filled with pride and a desire to conquer others. They dwelt carelessly and rejoiced in their pride saying, "I am and there is none beside me" (Zephaniah 2:15). But God is the great *I AM* (Exodus 3:14), and only He gets this distinctive title. Christ, the Word of the Old Testament, told the Pharisees "before Abraham was, I AM" (John 8:58). In their arrogance, these kingdoms never imagined anyone could best them, yet God said,

> *This is the rejoicing city that dwelt carelessly, that said in her heart, I am, and there is none beside me: how is she become a desolation, a place for beasts to lie down in! every one that passeth by her shall hiss, and wag his hand. (Zephaniah 2:15)*

The emotion of pride is twofold, and we've all felt both sides. One side is that swelling of joy over something our child accomplished, that wahoo feeling when we excel at a difficult task. Look what I did! But the other side of pride is where we go wrong. Forgetting that all our talent and blessings come directly from God. Forgetting that our excellence, our achievements, our wins are, of a truth, His. Dark pride drives us to shun lowly, unappreciated service to others; we glory in accolades instead. Infected with this side of pride, we refuse to forgive. (Why should we? We're not wrong.) Pride inflates our sense of worth and thinks we deserve more than what we've got. Our excellence, our achievements, our wins are ours. Look what *I* did! The pride of achievement can easily morph into arrogance, self-reliance, and an unteachable spirit. Pride knows better than God.

In Judah's day, God's punishment was imminent and bitter to those He spoke against. "The great day of the Lord is near, it is near, and hasteth greatly, even the voice of the day of the Lord: the mighty man shall cry there bitterly" (Zephaniah 1:14). Likewise, Christ's return and righteous judgment is imminent and will be bitter to the mighty and unprepared. Who are the mighty? Anyone great or small, rich or poor unwilling to yield to God. They are mighty in their own eyes, proud of their life apart from God. Who are the unprepared? Anyone claiming Christ's name but *settled on their lees.*

> *And it shall come to pass at that time, that I will search Jerusalem with candles, and punish the men that are settled on their lees: that say in their heart, The Lord will not do good, neither will he do evil.*
> *(Zephaniah 1:12)*

Lees are the sediment found at the bottom of wine vessels, the dregs that nobody wants to drink.[3] Many believers in Christ are settled on their lees, reclined upon the couch of self-delusion, and think, "I don't have to do anything because Christ did it for me on the cross." That is true, to a point. You can't do anything to earn salvation. You can't try to be really, really, good so God will look down and see your "goodness" and save you from His coming wrath. It doesn't work that way. Upon conversion, yes, we rest confident in Christ's work done for us on the cross. Yes, we rest in the merciful grace God drapes us in every day like a fine silken robe. But this rest is not a pardon to live as we please. This grace is not our excuse to sin as Paul explained in Romans 6:1–2. No. Christ paid our price; His sacrifice saves us. But we must get up and do the true work of a Christian—obey His Word. Obedience to Christ is doing, it is service to others and slaying of self, it is making righteous choices that reflect our love for Him. If we settle on our lees, we become careless. We become overconfident or lackadaisical in our calling, thinking God isn't judging us now or that God doesn't care what we do. Yet God said He will "render to every man according to his deeds" (Romans 2:6).

Matthew 25 warns that many believers will be unprepared for Christ's return. Like the foolish virgins, they wait for Him with unfilled lamps and think nothing of it. But lamps need oil to work. The oil of truth and knowledge, the oil of wisdom and discernment. Without these, we won't grow spiritually. What's so tragic is these people hold the vessel that God gave them but do nothing with it. They expect to join the Bridegroom without yielding their lives to His Spirit. They are called but not chosen (Matthew 22:14).

> *For the time is come that judgment must begin at the house of God: and if it first begin at us, what shall the end be of them that obey not the gospel of God? (1 Peter 4:17)*

## God's love and His judgments

God's love and His judgments are intertwined. He doesn't mete out punishment without warnings first. He sent hand-picked prophets to warn Israel and Judah in the days of old. He warns us today in the pages of Scripture we hold in our hands. Every morning God brings His judgment to light (Zephaniah 3:5).

After God's warnings went unheeded, God told Zephaniah in Zephaniah 1–6 He would punish Jerusalem because they

1. Kept the remnant of Baal, the god of Babylon Judah loved in their midst (1:4)
2. Tolerated the pagan and idolatrous priests (called *Chemarim* in the KJV) (1:4)

3. Swore by the Lord *and* by Malcham, a pagan god also known as Milcom or Molech (1:5)
4. Turned back from the Lord (they once followed!) (1:6)
5. Did not seek the Lord nor inquire of Him in their daily lives (1:6)

Instead of asking themselves why they were being punished so they could learn from it and seek God's forgiveness, the kingdom of Judah (and the kingdom of Israel before them) continued doing whatever was pleasing to them.

> *She obeyed not the voice; she received not correction; she trusted not in the Lord; she drew not near to her God. (Zephaniah 3:2)*

> *I said, Surely thou wilt fear me, thou wilt receive instruction; so their dwelling should not be cut off, howsoever I punished them: but they rose early, and corrupted all their doings. (Zephaniah 3:7)*

Judah wasn't being exclusive in their worship of God. They were mingling truth with falsehood. Mixing holy with profane.[4] Likewise, if we dabble in astrology, New Age ideology, Eastern Mysticism, witchcraft, tarot cards, the occult *and* think we can be a Christian too, we are mistaken. If we hold to the ideals of feminism and secularism, if we support abortion, eugenics, transgenderism, homosexuality, gay marriage *and* believe we can be a Christian too, we are blind to who Christ is. If we strive to be rich and covet what this world offers *and* want the blessings of God, we've got it all wrong. Our worship is not pure. We reduce Christ to another ism and ology that makes us feel good but doesn't have the power to change us or give us life. God's punishment for Judah's half-hearted dealings with Him, and especially for those who once knew him and turned back should give us pause. Peter spoke a similar warning in the New Testament.

> *For if after they have escaped the pollutions of the world*
> *through the knowledge of the Lord and Saviour Jesus*
> *Christ, they are again entangled therein, and overcome, the*
> *latter end is worse with them than the beginning.*
> *For it had been better for them not to have known the way*
> *of righteousness, than, after they have known it, to turn*
> *from the holy commandment delivered unto them.*
> *(2 Peter 2:20–21)*

## God prepares a sacrifice and a feast

In ancient Israel, animal sacrifice was the means by which unholy people could come before a holy God and be forgiven. It was a vivid example of how the shedding of blood is required for sin. Christ became that final sacrifice required for our sins and, if we live faithful to God, we stand before Him as holy and forgiven women. In Zephaniah 1:7, God made it clear to the inhabitants of Judah that *they* were the intended sacrifice, the animal chosen for slaughter because of their multitude of sins. God had prepared a sacrifice in Zephaniah's day and will prepare the final sacrifice in the "day of the Lord" of all nations and people who oppose Him. "Hold thy peace at the presence of the Lord God: for the day of the Lord is at hand: for the Lord hath prepared a sacrifice, he hath bid his guests" (Zephaniah 1:7).

God has invited us to attend His feast; what a blessed invitation. Are we ready? Many believers who've been invited will find themselves woefully unprepared and clothed in strange apparel (Zephaniah 1:8). Have we chosen the fabric of this world, the warp and woof of defilement? Are we draped in clothing we prefer but is abhorrent to God?

> *And when the king came in to see the guests, he saw there a man which had not on a wedding garment:*
> *And he saith unto him, Friend, how camest thou in hither not having a wedding garment? And he was speechless.*
> *Then said the king to the servants, Bind him hand and foot, and take him away, and cast him into outer darkness; there shall be weeping and gnashing of teeth.*
> *(Matthew 22:11–13)*

God warned Jerusalem that their day of the Lord would be a day of wrath, of trouble, of distress, and a "day of the trumpet" (Zephaniah 1:15–16). Trumpet calls were used in different ways in ancient times: to alert the people for assembly, to signal the approach of a festival, to prepare men for battle and their city for impending doom. The trumpet of alarm brought fear to the ancient world and will bring fear to the modern. The book of Revelation speaks of the seven trumpets of God that signal the destruction of wicked mankind and the all-encompassing triumph of Christ's kingdom (Revelation 11:15).

The phrases "the fire of my jealousy" and "the fire of his jealousy" are only found three times in the King James Version. Once in Ezekiel 36:5 and twice in Zephaniah.[5]

*Neither their silver nor their gold shall be able to deliver
them in the day of the Lord's wrath; but the whole land
shall be devoured by the **fire of his jealousy**: for he shall
make even a speedy riddance of all them that dwell in the
land. (Zephaniah 1:18, emphasis added)*

Like we learned in the book of Nahum, God is righteously
jealous for His people and His holy name. And Zephaniah
declared this fiery jealousy will scorch everything not covered
by it. But we have nothing to fear; we are shielded. His fire-
proof name protects us from His wrath like no amount of
earthly wealth the world trusts in (a pseudo shield at best) could
ever do.

In the book of Zephaniah, there is an astounding verse
guaranteed to uplift your weary woman's heart. The day we see
God in His kingdom, He will greet us with joyful singing.

*The Lord thy God in the midst of thee is mighty; he
will save, he will rejoice over thee with joy; he will rest
in his love, he will joy over thee with singing.
(Zephaniah 3:17)*

Like cheering for an exhausted runner in a marathon, our
moment of crossing will engender a torrent of gladness, an
enveloping love song—what a glorious sound that will be!—
from our God who has patiently waited to welcome us into
His rest.

# What's the story behind...?

*In the same day also will I punish all those that **leap on the threshold**, which fill their masters' houses with violence and deceit. (Zephaniah 1:9)*

Most Bible translations interpret the preposition *on* in the bolded phrase above as *over* instead, drawing the picture of people swiftly and arrogantly entering the house of the Lord without reverence and defiling it by their behavior. Other translations interpret this phrase as a reference to pagan worship practices similar to what is found in 1 Samuel 5:5.[6]

# Zephaniah notes

1. *Strong's* reference H6846, taken from H6845.
2. Moab and Ammon were the descendants of the incestuous offspring of Lot and his two daughters recorded in Genesis 19:36–38.
3. *Strong's* reference H8105.
4. See Ezekiel 22:26.
5. See also Zephaniah 3:8.
6. A.W. Workman, "Those Who Leap Over the Threshold," Entrusted to the Dirt (blog), September 17, 2020, accessed on April 23, 2025, https://entrustedtothedirt.com/2020/09/17/those-who-leap-over-the-threshold/.

# Haggai

*I will fill this house with glory*

In the book of Haggai, God bids we do three things: (1) consider our ways, (2) do the work He's put before us, and (3) be strong—do not fear. The phrase "consider your ways," or simply "consider," is written five times in this short, two-chapter book, making it an important keyword we need to rightly consider. When a word or phrase is repeated in a passage of the Bible, it's like a yellow highlighter or flashing arrow on the text giving us a clue to pay attention. Do we consider our ways? Do we align our words and actions with God's Word? Do we apply our hearts unto wisdom? God doesn't expect us to do what He asks by our own strength and power. He promises when we women step out in faith and obey Him, He will be with us. And Haggai spoke of this fluorescent promise more than once.

In the Old Testament books of Ezra and Nehemiah, the people of Judah were allowed to return from their captivity in Babylon and rebuild the temple at Jerusalem by the order of Cyrus, the new king of Babylon. The prophet Haggai, mentioned in Ezra 5:1 and 6:14, was one of many Jews who made the exultant journey back to their homeland. But in the opening of the book of Haggai, years had passed, another Babylonian king, Darius, was on the throne, and the temple was still not finished. Trials, distractions, and their own complacency had gotten in the way of completing the work. They kept making excuses that the time wasn't right (Haggai 1:2) yet they had time to build their own homes.

> *Then came the word of the Lord by Haggai the prophet, saying,*
> *Is it time for you, O ye, to dwell in your cieled houses, and this house lie waste? (Haggai 1:3–4)*

The returning Israelites had plenty of time for their own business, but their service to God was lacking. They worked hard for physical gain, but it was like putting money in a bag full of holes (Haggai 1:6). God tells them why in verse 9.

> *Ye looked for much, and, lo, it came to little; and when ye brought it home, I did blow upon it. Why? saith the Lord of hosts. Because of mine house that is waste, and ye run every man unto his own house. (Haggai 1:9)*

They looked for much and got little in return because God took it away to wake them up. He told them to consider their ways (Haggai 1:5, 7). He was asking them, "Where is your heart in the matter? Why do you think you can prosper without Me?"

*I am the vine, ye are the branches: He that abideth in me, and I in him, the same bringeth forth much fruit: for without me ye can do nothing. (John 15:5)*

We all have work to do. God has specific assignments for each of us while we're here. We are wives, mothers, friends, teachers, artists, caregivers, business owners, and organizers extraordinaire. But we run around frantically trying to do "all the things" and forget to put God first. We set out to do great things without consulting Him, without asking that His will be done. God wants our hearts fixed on Him (Psalm 57:7). Our minds set on things above (Colossians 3:2). And He wants whatever work we do to be done for His glory (1 Corinthians 10:31). When we work with that goal in mind, we cannot help but prosper. But God was not central to the Israelite's pursuits. What they did, they did for themselves; their works were unclean.

*Then answered Haggai, and said, So is this people, and so is this nation before me, saith the Lord; and so is every work of their hands; and that which they offer there is unclean. (Haggai 2:14)*

Therefore God stopped the rain and the harvest, brought drought upon man and beast, and sent Haggai to implore Zerubbabel, the appointed governor, and Joshua, the high priest, and all the people to consider their ways and get back to His work. And guess what? They listened! They feared the Lord and began the work with renewed purpose, trusting God for the provisions. God stirred up their spirits, gave them confidence in the task before them, and spoke through Haggai this heart-warming message: I am with you (Haggai 1:13).

## Zerubbabel and Christ

Haggai chapter 2 praises Zerubbabel for his obedience and likens him to a signet. A signet was an emblem, seal, or signature ring unique to the king. It was used as an authority marker, like a signature on an official document or check. Anyone who saw the signet accepted the item as a genuine document of the king.

> *In that day, saith the Lord of hosts, will I take thee, O Zerubbabel, my servant, the son of Shealtiel, saith the Lord, and will make thee as a signet: for I have chosen thee, saith the Lord of hosts. (Haggai 2:23)*

Zerubbabel was born in Babylon, far from his ancestors' heritage in Israel, but he was not forgotten. Zerubbabel was a descendant of David and was included in the lineage of Christ. He is mentioned in the New Testament (spelled *Zorobabel*) in Matthew 1:12 and Luke 3:27. The story of Zerubbabel in the book of Haggai has a striking parallel with Jesus Christ and who we are in Him.

| | |
|---|---|
| 1) Zerubbabel glorified God with obedience and honor. | Christ glorified God, the Father, with obedience and honor. |
| 2) Zerubbabel oversaw the temple construction made by hands. | We are the temple of God made without hands (1 Corinthians 3:16). |
| 3) Under Zerubbabel's rule, there was peace and prosperity for Jerusalem. | Under Christ's rule, there will be final and lasting peace and prosperity for the new Jerusalem (Revelation 21:2). |
| 4) God chose Zerubbabel. He became a signet in the hand of God because of his obedience and faithful service. | God, the Father, chose His Son, Jesus Christ, because of His obedience and faithful sacrifice, to redeem us. Christ is the perfect signet wielding kingly authority over all the earth (Matthew 28:18). |

As obedient and faithful Christian women, happy and blessed are we to be chosen by God to live in eternity with Him. We were chosen even before we were faithful. "According as he hath chosen us in him before the foundation of the world, that we should be holy and without blame before him in love" (Ephesians 1:4).

God is referred to as the *Lord of hosts*, or *God of hosts*, nearly 280 times in the Old Testament. In this little book of Haggai, "Lord of hosts" is mentioned fourteen times.

*Lift up your heads, O ye gates; even lift them up, ye everlasting doors; and the King of glory shall come in. Who is this King of glory? The Lord of hosts, he is the King of glory. Selah. (Psalm 24:9–10)*

The word *hosts* means "mass of persons; army, or company" and refers to God's innumerable body of angels.[1] They are His flaming ministers of fire sent to assist His children and to execute God's judgment at His will. God warned Zerubbabel He would shake the nations and overthrow their kingdoms (Haggai 2:6, 22), and He means to do this a final time. These nations and kingdoms and people around the world who want nothing to do with God and His righteousness will soon meet this Lord of hosts. Their desire to be autonomous, unaccountable, and to be their own god will one day fight against Christ at His return to their own destruction. "And I will shake all nations, and the desire of all nations shall come: and I will fill this house with glory, saith the Lord of hosts" (Haggai 2:7). Christ will overthrow all kingdoms. This nation, and every other nation, will cease to exist at His return (Daniel 2:44).

## This latter house

God told the prophet Haggai to ask the older residents of Jerusalem if they remembered what the first temple looked like. And then God gave this declaration:

> *The glory of this latter house shall be greater than of the former, saith the Lord of hosts: and in this place will I give peace, saith the Lord of hosts. (Haggai 2:9)*

The physical temple was undoubtedly glorious to behold, but the spiritual house is greater still. *We* are this latter house. We women are part of God's household. And because of His love toward us who obey Him, we will be filled to overflowing with glory, like a fine basin cascading with splendor, joy spilling playfully at our feet. When your life is weighed down by the relentless downpour of trials, a suffering that seeps through the ceiling of your mind—take heart. For as much as you've lost, had taken away, or had to give up with tears for Christ's name and the Father's will, you will receive a hundredfold in godly riches.

It is our faith in God who cannot lie that patiently waits to suffuse us with His peace. As His cherished daughters, He desires to give us health for our sickness, safety for our fear, and prosperity for our utter destitution, making us whole and complete. He will repay our debts, restore our losses, and all will be well with our souls. Because this latter house is filled with the King of glory, we can take comfort in the lavish love of a Father who desires to lift the boulders of sorrows we carry and exchange our cumbersome load with His abundant glory instead. Hallelujah!

In the book of Haggai, God implored the Israelites to pay attention to what they were doing and to remember the way things were before. He essentially said, "Remember when you hoped for more and got less? Now, because of your obedience, prepare yourselves for more than you ever thought possible."

> *Is the seed yet in the barn? yea, as yet the vine, and the*
> *fig tree, and the pomegranate, and the olive tree, hath not*
> *brought forth: from this day will I bless you.*
> *(Haggai 2:19)*

We, too, need to consider where we came from before our devotion to Christ and where we are now. We need to consider the answered prayers of our past, the provisions that God blessed us with when everything seemed impossible. God wants us to be thankful women ready and willing to receive His blessings even if these blessings are different from what we would choose for ourselves. The silver is mine, the gold is mine, says God (Haggai 2:8). If everything belongs to God, then why do we fear we won't have enough? He is our Father, and we are His daughters, and He freely gives of His provisions without hoarding or favoritism. He provides the raw materials of faith, virtue, knowledge, temperance, patience, godliness, brotherly kindness, and love (2 Peter 1:5–8) to get the work done. All we need to do is ask (and maybe change our perspective on what think we really need). Every day is a day to consider. "To day," as written in Hebrews 3:13–15, is the right time, the right day to listen, to love, to soften our hearts toward God. "To day" is the day to uplift the lonely and desperate brothers and sisters in Christ and urge them to continue the good fight of faith. When we listen to God, as Zerubbabel, Joshua, and all the inhabitants of Jerusalem did, God promises us peace and blessings.

We can be strong and fearless women as we do our work because God says repeatedly I am with you (Haggai 1:13–14; 2:4–5). But forging ahead and doing the work God gives us isn't easy. Fears and doubts pop up when we submit to our husbands, teach our children, serve our communities, give away our time and money, or begin a project that's neither pleasant nor guaranteed to succeed. We might try to do these things on our own strength, maybe even prosper for a time, but eventually, we will fail. Obedience to God, honoring His name through our actions, and ignoring the world and all that goes with it is only possible when God's strength supersedes our own. And here's the thing: when we trust and obey God in the midst of our fears, godly strength takes over and steadily replaces each doubt, hesitation, and worry with His peace. The phrase "fear not" is found seventy-four times in the King James Bible and the phrase "do not be afraid" twenty-nine times. Wow! What a huge yellow highlighter across our hearts. God doesn't ever want us to forget that when we trust Him, He is there.

## What's the story behind...?

*If one bear **holy flesh** in the skirt of his garment, and with*
*his skirt do touch bread, or pottage, or wine, or oil, or any*
*meat, shall it be holy? And the priests answered and said,*
*No. (Haggai 2:12)*

The "holy flesh" was the meat of sacrificial animals. Because the
meat was dedicated to God, it was holy and thereby, the garment
used to transport it became holy. The "skirt" was the pockets or
flaps of cloth on the priest's robes where they might carry the
meat for burnt offerings or to cook for their own consumption.
But if the priests touched common things along the way, the
garment did make those things holy. The sanctifying power
extended directly to the first thing touched. Like the phrase,
"God has no grandchildren,"[2] we are holy because we have
been touched by God's Spirit, a one-to-one encounter, but we
can't make someone else holy. God has to directly touch them.

# Haggai notes

1. *Strong's* reference H6635.
2. Reinhard Bonnke Quotes. BrainyQuote.com, accessed April 24, 2025, https://www.brainyquote.com/quotes/ reinhard_bonnke_921280.

11

# Zechariah

*And the house of David shall be as God*

Image you enter a room, and there before you sits an absurdly long wooden table polished to gleaming. Ornate silver platters laden with mouth-watering delicacies crowd its surface. This is the book of Zechariah. You feast on one chapter, but the next chapter has yet more tasty morsels to sample. This book is the longest of the twelve Minor Prophets and full of tantalizing imagery, hearty admonition, and sweet, satisfying promises of peace and prosperity for those who hold tightly to the Branch. Jesus Christ is this Branch who "shall bear the glory, and shall sit and rule upon his throne" (Zechariah 6:12). He is the strong stock that bears our sins, buds forth truth and righteousness, and blossoms hope in the core of our being.

*Behold, the days come, saith the Lord, that I will raise*
*unto David a righteous Branch, and a King shall reign*
*and prosper, and shall execute judgment and justice in*
*the earth. (Jeremiah 23:5)*

Zechariah prophesied, along with his partner prophet, Haggai, during Judah's return to Jerusalem from their seventy-year captivity in Babylon. As we learned in the book of Haggai, the temple reconstruction was still delayed, and God had asked His idol-distracted, self-satisfied children why their houses were complete and His was not. Both the books of Haggai and Zechariah mention Zerubbabel and Joshua and their favor with God for their obedience. But throughout this book, God showed fantastic visions of the end times to Zechariah (some of which are head-scratchers but were put there for a reason and deserve our attention). God also proclaimed to Zechariah His faithful promises to overturn our afflictions and lift us up like a regal banner and polished stones in His royal crown for all the world to see.[1]

*And the Lord their God shall save them in that day as*
*the flock of his people: for they shall be as the stones of a*
*crown, lifted up as an ensign upon his land.*
*For how great is his goodness, and how great is his*
*beauty! corn shall make the young men cheerful, and new*
*wine the maids. (Zechariah 9:16–17)*

We are afflicted people now, outcasts from an unworthy world (Hebrews 11:38), and prisoners of hope (Zechariah 9:12), but that will soon change at Christ's return. God has not forgotten our pain and our struggles. He will avenge and make right all the evil done to us by those who thought they would escape accountability. Zechariah was the righteous man Christ mentioned in Matthew 23:35 and Luke 11:51 whom the fathers of the scribes and Pharisees had murdered.

> *Wherefore, behold, I send unto you prophets, and wise men, and scribes: and some of them ye shall kill and crucify; and some of them shall ye scourge in your synagogues, and persecute them from city to city:*
> *That upon you may come all the righteous blood shed upon the earth, from the blood of righteous Abel unto the blood of Zacharias son of Barachias, whom ye slew between the temple and the altar. (Matthew 23:34–35)*

God remembers all injustices; He will repay. Zechariah's death was not forgotten by God those five hundred years between the book of Zechariah and when Christ spoke in Matthew. Zechariah's name (spelled *Zacharias* in Matthew) means "God remembers"![2]

Note: In Matthew 23:35, the margin notes in the King James Version for the death of Zechariah take you to 2 Chronicles 24:21 where a Zechariah, the son of Jehoiada, is murdered in the court of the temple. This seems like it might be the same person, but the timeline is wrong. In Zechariah 1:1, Zechariah is recorded as being the son of Berechiah (spelled *Barachias* in the New Testament), who was the son of Iddo (Zechariah's grandfather). Although the name Zechariah and the manner of deaths are similar, this is clearly not the same person. The incident recorded in 2 Chronicles is roughly three centuries before the book of Zechariah was written. It's good to remember that footnotes and cross-references, although helpful, are not divinely inspired but were added by men who sometimes make mistakes, as they did here. Christ, who made no mistake, was referring to the author of this book when He lambasted the scribes and Pharisees in the book of Matthew.

## Zechariah's visions

Thankfully, for Zechariah and for us, an angel was nearby to explain the meaning of the visions Zechariah saw:

1.  A man on a red horse, and other horses red, speckled, and white. Answer: These are angels that God sent to walk to and fro on the earth (1:8–11).
2.  Four horns. Answer: These are the powerful nations that brought down Judah, Israel, and the city of Jerusalem (1:18–19).
3.  Four carpenters. Answer: These are those who will take down the four horns (1:20–21).
4.  A man with a measuring line. Answer: This is an angel who measured Jerusalem and declared that Jerusalem would be a city without walls for the multitude of inhabitants (2:1–6).
5.  A golden candlestick with seven lamps and seven pipes. Answer: In the Bible, seven represents perfection. The oil and the light from these lamps represent God's Spirit, power, holiness, knowledge, and truth flowing into us, His church. The seven lamps are the seven eyes of God which run to and fro through the whole earth (4:2–10).

6. Two olive trees. Answer: These are the two anointed ones or witnesses (angels sent by God[3]) who will prophesy throughout the whole earth for three-and-a-half years at the beginning of the tribulation (4:11–14).

7. A flying roll [scroll]. Answer: This is the volume of God's accounts against wickedness that will sweep through the land and convict the thief and the liar (5:1–4).

8. An ephah [a dry measure similar to a bushel], a talent of lead [a weight, circle, coin], and one woman sitting within the ephah. Answer: The woman represents wickedness covered by a heavy lead lid (5:6–8).

9. Two women with wings carrying the ephah to Shinar. Answer: Wickedness is taken and settled in the valley of Babylon, the seat of all false religions (5:9–11).[4]

10. Four chariots flying between two brass mountains. Answer: These chariots are four spirits or winds (angels) sent by God over the earth. The two brass mountains are not specifically explained,[5] but mountains often represent kingdoms and brass often represents strength and judgment in the Bible, so here they could represent the time between the earthly kingdom and the coming spiritual kingdom of Israel (6:1–5).[6]

In Zechariah 3:9 and 4:10, God speaks of seven eyes on a stone. Revelation 5:6 speaks of the Lamb which was slain having seven eyes. The Lamb is Christ and the eyes are the seven Spirits of God. But what are the seven Spirits of God exactly? There's no definitive answer, but in Isaiah chapter eleven we learn this:

*And there shall come forth a rod out of the stem of Jesse,*
*and a Branch shall grow out of his roots:*
*And the spirit of the Lord shall rest upon him, the spirit*
*of wisdom and understanding, the spirit of counsel and*
*might, the spirit of knowledge and of the fear of the Lord.*
*(Isaiah 11:1–2)*

Our Lord Jesus Christ is the cornerstone the builders rejected.[7] He is the stone with seven eyes. He is the one who shall bear the glory and shall sit and rule upon His throne as a priest and counselor of peace (Zechariah 6:13). While these visions seem random, like a weird dream that makes no sense, they all have meaning and purpose. Zechariah's visions point to God's hand in everything. By God's command, angels roam the whole earth. God keeps track of the wicked deeds and will soon punish the evildoers. Jerusalem will be a city of peace, full to brimming, and God, the glory within her. The seat of paganism began with the tower of Babel (men trying to be their own god) in the heart of Babylon, and Babylon's worldly influence will be utterly destroyed by Christ's second coming. God's two witnesses are coming to speak truth to an obstinate world, and God's perfection (seven lamps, seven bowls, seven eyes, seven Spirits) will reign triumphant on the earth.

## Four prophecies fulfilled

The only Old Testament book to foretell that Jesus Christ would ride into Jerusalem on a donkey was Zechariah. Two other well-known prophecies fulfilled by Christ in the New Testament were first written by the prophet Zechariah:

| | |
|---|---|
| *Rejoice greatly, O daughter of Zion; shout, O daughter of Jerusalem: behold, thy King cometh unto thee: he is just, and having salvation;* **lowly,** *and* **riding upon an ass, and** *upon* **a colt the foal of an ass.** *(Zechariah 9:9)* | *Tell ye the daughter of Sion, Behold, thy King cometh unto thee,* **meek,** *and* **sitting upon an ass,** *and* **a colt the foal of an ass.** *(Matthew 21:5)* |
| *Awake, O sword, against my shepherd, and against the man that is my fellow, saith the Lord of hosts: smite the shepherd, and* **the sheep shall be scattered:** *and I will turn mine hand upon the little ones. (Zechariah 13:7)* | *Then saith Jesus unto them, All ye shall be offended because of me this night: for it is written, I will smite the shepherd, and* **the sheep of the flock shall be scattered** *abroad. (Matthew 26:31)[8]* |
| *And I will pour upon the house of David, and upon the inhabitants of Jerusalem, the spirit of grace and of supplications: and they shall* **look upon me whom they have pierced.** *(Zechariah 12:10)* | *For these things were done, that the scripture should be fulfilled, A bone of him shall not be broken. And again another scripture saith, They shall* **look on him whom they pierced.** *(John 19:36–37)* |

The final prophecy written in Zechariah and fulfilled in the the New Testament is found in chapter 11. God told Zechariah to feed the flock of slaughter, so named because the shepherds (e.g., priests) spiritually killed their flock for profit and blessed the Lord while doing it (Zechariah 11:5). He also told him to ask these religious leaders to pay him what they thought he was worth to them, and they gave him thirty pieces of silver—the equivalent of the price of an injured slave.[9] This was the exact price given to Judas Iscariot to betray Christ.

> *Then one of the twelve, called Judas Iscariot, went unto the chief priests,*
> *And said unto them, What will ye give me, and I will deliver him unto you? And they covenanted with him for thirty pieces of silver. (Matthew 26:14–15)*

A bit of a mystery is found in Matthew 27:9–10. Jesus Christ says it was Jeremiah the prophet that spoke of the thirty pieces of silver being His value in the eyes of the children of Israel. But no actual verse in Jeremiah exists where this is written. (Christ did say Jeremiah had spoken this, not written this.) It could be Zechariah remembered what others who had heard Jeremiah speak a generation before said and wanted to preserve it. Another explanation for the confusion might be this: the Old Testament books were in a different order than they appear in our Bibles now. Scripture was divided into three parts, (1) the Law, which contained the five books of Moses; (2) the Prophets, which contained the former and latter prophets (the former began at Joshua and the latter began at Jeremiah); and lastly, (3) the Writings. Hence, the passage in Zechariah that was in that latter book of the Prophets might be cited under the umbrella name of Jeremiah.[10]

Taking on the role of a shepherd, God told Zechariah to take two staves (plural for a staff used for walking or guiding a flock) and name one *Beauty* and the other *Bands*. The staff Beauty represented Israel, His chosen and beloved people. God told Zechariah to cut it in two. This depicted the severing of the covenant God had with Israel. The old covenant was removed to usher in a far superior one that would be established after the death and resurrection of Jesus Christ.

The staff Bands was also cut in two and represented the breaking of the bonds of brotherhood between Israel and Judah. Although Judah and Israel had already been separated for centuries by this point, the breaking of this staff vividly showed that the binders of exclusivity the physical tribes of Israel and Judah had were broken so that God's salvation would be open to any nation who chose the one true Shepherd.

> *But he is a Jew, which is one inwardly; and circumcision is that of the heart, in the spirit, and not in the letter; whose praise is not of men, but of God. (Romans 2:29)*

> *That the Gentiles should be fellowheirs, and of the same body, and partakers of his promise in Christ by the gospel. (Ephesians 3:6)*

Most prophecies found throughout the Bible have dual purposes as Zechariah 13:8–9 shows. They inform the people it was originally written for with warnings and admonitions, and they also speak to future generations like us.

> *And it shall come to pass, that in all the land, saith the Lord,* **two parts therein shall be cut off and die;** *but the third shall be left therein.*
> *And* **I will bring the third part through the fire,** *and will refine them as silver is refined, and will try them a gold is tried: they shall call on my name, and I will hear them: I will say, It is my people: and they shall say,* **The Lord is my God.** *(Zechariah 13:8–9, emphasis added)*

Zechariah's prophecy foretold what happened in AD 70 when the Romans laid siege to Jerusalem and approximately two-thirds of the people died or were enslaved. The remaining third went through difficult times by the hand of God for their good. We can also apply this prophecy to our end-time's future. Churches often overlook Christ's words that many are called, and few are chosen (Matthew 22:14). Many people in the world have been invited to the wedding feast, given a choice at some point in their lives to follow and obey God. Many more will be called from now till the great tribulation. But of these many, when God's kingdom does come, they will be standing there speechless, in the wrong attire, still unwilling to accept God as their savior (Matthew 22:12). Still unwilling to say, "The Lord is my God." They will fight for their right to be autonomous and die because their hearts and minds were never changed. Even those who thought themselves Christian, like the foolish virgins at the Bridegroom's door who had in their possession the lamp of their calling but didn't use it, will not be allowed inside.

We all know what it's like to have our faith tested. We Christ followers living through the harrowing end times will have our faith tested more than ever before. But this testing, this refining fire, is necessary to burn away the dross of falsehood that is our reliance on the world and our own stubborn ways. God says in Zechariah 13:9 He will bring us through the fire. He will be right there with us through it all. God's purification process for His beloved children will result in our praise, honor, and glory at Christ's return (1 Peter 1:7).

## Joshua, Christ typified

One of several visions in this vision-packed book shows Joshua, the son of Josedec, who was the high priest in Jerusalem at that time, standing by an angel of the Lord, and Satan standing right by to accuse him. Satan, whose name means *adversary*,[11] never stops trying to provoke us to sin and to accuse us. It is a constant battle. But he has no power over us unless we act on our temptations. James 4:7 says, "Submit yourselves therefore to God. Resist the devil, and he will flee from you."

God told Zechariah to direct the priests in making crowns of gold and silver and to place them upon the head of Joshua saying, "Behold, the man whose name is the BRANCH; and he shall grow up out of his place, and he shall build the temple of the Lord" (Zechariah 6:12). The name *Joshua* means "Jehovah saved"[12] and is the Hebrew name for Jesus! Ah, here in the book of Zechariah, we learn that Joshua, the high priest, represented the ultimate high priest of God, Christ Jesus. It is Christ who builds the temple. And we are that temple filled with the Spirit of God (1 Corinthians 3:16).

Zechariah's vision continued with an image of Joshua in filthy clothes. The filth represented humanity's total depravity and wickedness Christ bore to the cross. He took on our sins so we could become clean. Christ lovingly removes our filthy garments, encrusted with the sins that so easily beset us (Hebrews 12:1), and replaces them with His regal garments of splendor.

> *I will greatly rejoice in the Lord, my soul shall be joyful in my God; for he hath clothed me with the garments of salvation, he hath covered me with the robe of righteousness, as a bridegroom decketh himself with ornaments, and as a bride adorneth herself with her jewels. (Isaiah 61:10)*

In order to be draped in these new clothes, God put forth these simple dos and don'ts in the book of Zechariah.

**Do:**
- Speak the truth to your neighbor (8:16).
- Defend the truth and stand for peace in your home and nation (8:16, 19).
- Judge righteously (7:9).
- Show mercy and compassion to all (7:9).

**Don't:**
- Harbor ill will or hatred for your neighbor (7:10; 8:17).
- Take advantage of the widow, the fatherless, the stranger, or the poor (7:10).
- Love a lie, which God hates (8:17).

These *don'ts* come from the spirit of Babylon and God commands us to separate ourselves from her. "Wherefore come out from among them, and be ye separate, saith the

Lord, and touch not the unclean thing; and I will receive you" (2 Corinthians 6:17). But the people Zechariah spoke to didn't want to separate themselves and refused to yield to these straightforward admonitions. Instead they "pulled away ... and stopped their ears ... [and] made their hearts as an adamant stone" (Zechariah 7:11–12).[13] Adamant about self-rule, adamant against softening themselves in obedience to God. This was why God had "scattered them with a whirlwind among all the nations they knew not" years before (Zechariah 7:14). God refused to hear their cries of distress then because they refused to hear the cries of the prophets God sent to warn them. And years later, they were repeating the same adamant cycle. But true to our merciful God, Zechariah was filled with hope and promise that Jerusalem would one day be called a city of truth and old and young alike would find peace and prosperity within her walls (Zechariah 8:1–8). The former days of sorrow and fasting would turn to joy and feasting, and all nations would come to seek the Lord of hosts in Jerusalem. God would be forever with us. (Zechariah 8:19–23).

Even if our souls are willing, these simple dos and don'ts are not so simple to live out. Our transformation into the likeness of Christ is a lifelong endeavor and impossible on our own strength. God wants our willing and pliable hearts, and He gives us His Spirit, His power, to accomplish these things.

> *Then he answered and spake unto me, saying, This is the word of the Lord unto Zerubbabel, saying, Not by might, nor by power, but by my spirit, saith the Lord of hosts. (Zechariah 4:6)*

God declared that Zerubbabel, the appointed governor of Jerusalem, would finish rebuilding the temple (Zechariah 4:9). But God wanted him and his men to know they would not accomplish this deed by their own strength, but by His. This goes for us too. If we try to build anything without God in the forefront of our minds, without asking if it's His will, we will struggle, and ultimately, fail. It is God who does the heavy lifting. He provides His Spirit and gives us the gift of faith. Without God, we can do nothing (John 15:5).

> *For by grace are ye saved through faith; and that not of*
> *yourselves: it is the gift of God:*
> *Not of works, lest any man should boast.*
> *For we are his workmanship, created in Christ Jesus unto*
> *good works, which God hath before ordained that we*
> *should walk in them. (Ephesians 2:8–10)*

We women have to start at the beginning somewhere—in our faith walks, our marriages, our families, and our seedling enterprises. It can be discouraging to see someone else excel in the areas we want to excel in but haven't yet. God speaks of this frustration in Zechariah 4:10, "For who hath despised the day of small things? for they shall rejoice." There is no reason to despair of our hard beginnings or our seemingly small gains, because whether our progress is frustratingly sloth-paced or not, it is God who accomplishes what He wants in us and for us. Our definition of success is not the same as God's. It's certainly not going to look like the world's version nor will it look like another Christian sister's. Her path and yours lead to the same destination, but God has chosen your path with its soul-stretching, faith-building contours unique to you. Any dreams and goals you despise because they stay small might be exactly what God intended; He has better things in mind. When we accept this, we can and will rejoice.

> *Being confident of this very thing, that he which hath begun a good work in you will perform it until the day of Jesus Christ. (Philippians 1:6)*

## In that day

As already mentioned in the commentary on Hosea, when the Bible refers to Jesus Christ's second coming, you'll find phrases like "in that day," "at that day," "the day of the Lord," and "in the last days." The book of Zechariah uses one of these phrases over twenty times. The promises of God toward us are many regarding His coming kingdom. We, as true believers in Christ, are the spiritual Jerusalem; we are the beloved spiritual nation of Israel that will be the inheritors of all the glory, mercy, righteousness, and love God has reserved for us.

- *In that day*, God will defend Jerusalem, and it will be called a city of truth (Zechariah 8:3).
- *In that day*, God will destroy all nations that come up against Jerusalem with a consuming plague (Zechariah 12:9; 14:12).[14]
- *In that day*, God will cut off the names of the idols. Anything that brought us confusion, any object or ideology that defiled us, that caused us to sin, won't be remembered anymore. He will remove the prophets and

unclean spirits from the land (Zechariah 13:2). Once Christ returns, His very presence will fill and fulfill all things, negating the need for prophecy.

- *In that day*, we who are weak (and all of us are, whether physically, mentally, or spiritually) will be as King David (Zechariah 12:8).

- *In that day*, we will have great cause to sing because Christ said, "I will dwell in the midst of thee" (Zechariah 2:10).

- *In that day*, there will be no more night (Zechariah 14:7; Isaiah 60:19–20), and living water shall flow out from the temple, the throne of God (Zechariah 14:8; Joel 3:18; Revelation 22:1). Christ is that Living Water (Jeremiah 2:13; 17:13). Not only will He consume the darkness with His light but slack forever our thirst with His living water.

- *In that day*, many nations (people not yet called who survive the tribulation) will be joined to the Lord, and He shall call them His people (Zechariah 2:11; 8:11; Micah 4:1–3). In Zechariah 8:23, we read that ten men from different nations will entreat a Jew (a believer in Christ, most likely a resurrected spirit being) to let them go with him (to guide and teach them the knowledge of God) because they know God is with him.

- *In that day*, everything that exists from the mundane to the highly-regarded items will be "HOLINESS TO THE LORD" (Zechariah 14:20; Exodus 28:36).

The very last sentence in this monumental "minor" book of prophecy is intriguing. "In that day there shall be no more the Canaanite in the house of the Lord of hosts" (Zechariah 14:21). At first glance, we might assume Canaanite is referring to a physical nationality. The first mention of Canaan appears in Genesis 9:18.[15] Canaan was the son of Ham from which came the pagan cities of Babylon and Sodom and Gomorrah. Ham was the son of Noah who defiled his own father. God cursed Canaan, the descendants of Ham, but since Jesus Christ cleared the way for all Gentiles to be a part of his fold (even one of Christ's apostles was a Canaanite[16]), *Canaanite* must be referring to a moral type, the very antithesis of what God wants Israel to be. A Canaanite, in this verse in Zechariah, is a people set on rebellion against God's rule and authority. God wants us to purge our Canaanite hearts and be welcomed into His glorious kingdom where

nothing hurts or causes fear,
nothing makes us sick or causes tears,
where evil is nowhere to be found,
and true peace and prosperity abound.

# What's the story behind...?

*Should I **weep in the fifth month**, separating myself, as I have done these so many years? (Zechariah 7:3)*

Why did people of Jerusalem ask the priests this? What was the significance of the fifth month? The fifth month was a memorial of remembrance for the destruction of Jerusalem when Nebuzaradan, the Babylonian general under Nebuchadnezzar, burned Jerusalem and the temple, killing some of their leaders and dragging the rest to Babylon leaving the poor to tend the fields (2 Kings 25:8–9; Jeremiah 1:3; 52:12–16). Since the temple was being restored under Zerubbabel, they wanted to know if they should continue to mourn.

God's response to their question was a question for them, "When ye fasted and mourned in the fifth and seventh month,[17] even those seventy years, did ye at all fast unto me, even to me?" (Zechariah 7:5).

The Jews in Zechariah's day grieved for these tragedies, but their mourning was more out of self-pity and the loss of their way of life, than it was for mourning why God allowed the conquest in the first place—their repeated disobedience and lack of reverence to God.

# Zechariah notes

1. See also Isaiah 62:3.
2. *Strong's* reference H2148.
3. See Revelation 11:4.
4. See Revelation 17:5.
5. Another possible explanation is found in Zechariah 14:4
    which says that at Christ's return, He shall stand on the
    Mount of Olives fighting the nations that fought
    against Him, and the Mount shall split in two creating
    a great valley.
6. "Four Chariots From Between Two Mountains of Bronze,"
    commentary on Zechariah 6, Beyond Today,
    UCG.org, accessed April 24, 2025, https://
    www.ucg.org/bible-study-tools/bible-commentary/
    bible-commentary-zechariah-6.
7. See Psalm 118:22; Matthew 21:42; Mark 12:10; Luke 29:17;
    Acts 4:11; and 1 Peter 2:4–8.
8. See also Mark 14:27.
9. See Exodus 21:32.
10. "Matthew 27:9," commentary from *John Gill's Exposition of
    the Bible*, Bible Study Tools, accessed on April 24,
    2025, https://www.biblestudytools.com/
    commentaries/gills-exposition-of-the-bible/matthew-
    27-9.html#a.
11. *Strong's* reference H7854.
12. *Strong's* reference H3091. See also G2424.
13. *Strong's* reference H8086: *pricking*; a *thorn*; (for its ability to
    scratch) a *gem* (like the diamond).

14. Zechariah 14:12 may be eluding to chemical warfare.

15. *Strong's* reference H3667: *humiliated.*

16. See Matthew 10:4 and Mark 3:28.

17. The seventh month was a memorial for the murder of
     Gedaliah (Jeremiah 41:1–2). He was a Jew whom
     Nebuchadnezzar appointed governor over the
     remaining Jews left in Jerusalem after Nebuchadnezzar
     conquered them two months previous. God had
     allowed the conquest and the appointment of
     Gedaliah. But a rival prince of Jerusalem, Ishmael, the
     son of Nethaniah, decided he should be ruler instead
     and conspired with ten of his men to kill Gedaliah, and
     with trickery, betrayed Gedaliah and killed him (2
     Kings 25:25). But this act did not give him the
     kingdom. He ended up fleeing for his life to Ammon.

# Malachi

*For I am the Lord, I change not*

The book of Malachi was written fifty years after the missions of Haggai and Zechariah had ended. By the time Malachi began to prophesy, eighty-six years had passed since Zerubbabel and Joshua joyfully rebuilt the temple at Jerusalem, and once again, the people had grown weary in serving God. Malachi records the lack of fear the people of Jerusalem had for God. Their sacrificial offerings were laced with contempt, yet they wondered why God was displeased. They couldn't fool Him with their half-hearted, lukewarm offerings. Nor can we.

*So then because thou art lukewarm, and neither cold nor hot, I will spue thee out of my mouth. (Revelation 3:16)*

In Malachi, when God called out the sins of the priests and all the people, He repeated the phrase "Yet ye say," or "Ye say" thirteen times. He knew what their retort would be before they formed the words. He knew all their excuses, all their complaints and challenges, their doubtful questionings, their derisions based on their own corrupt feelings and judgments. Like the Israelites before us, we often look at life through the lens of our own standards, our own judgments, and not from God's. We see with dull eyes. God's judgment against Esau in Malachi 1:3, "I have hated Esau, and laid his mountains and his heritage waste" might seem harsh or unfair, but God knew what He was doing when He chose Jacob from the womb of Rebekah. He knew what Esau's future character and the later nation of Edom would be. Life might seem unfair, but when we trust God in everything, our vision becomes clearer. We have fewer "Yet ye say" moments. Things that don't make sense now can be handed to God with complete faith that He does, indeed, know what He's doing.

In Malachi chapter 1, God appealed to Jerusalem's common sense by asking the people if a son honors his father and a servant his master, and if I am your Father, then where is my honor? If I am your Master, where is my respect? He specifically called out the priests for their hypocrisy. "O priests, that despise my name. And ye say, Wherein have we despised thy name?" (Malachi 1:6). Once again, God knew their excuses and counterpoints. They despised God by how they lived and what they spoke and what they taught. They regarded the table of the Lord as contemptible, as polluted. They had no reverence or thankfulness in serving Him. They offered subpar sacrifices and expected God to be pleased.

*And if ye offer the blind for sacrifice, is it not evil? and if*
*ye offer the lame and sick, is it not evil? offer it now unto*
*thy governor; will he be pleased with thee, or accept thy*
*person? saith the Lord of hosts. (Malachi 1:8)*

They didn't offer second-rate gifts to their esteemed leaders
because that would have been an affront to the recipient and an
embarrassment to them. Yet they did it with God. They were,
in fact, robbing God with their inferior sacrifices. "Will a man
rob God? Yet ye have robbed me. But ye say, Wherein have
we robbed thee? In tithes and offerings" (Malachi 3:8). How do
we rob God of tithes and offerings now that the Levitical priest-
hood has been fulfilled in Christ? We do this by (a) holding back
from trusting God to direct our lives, afraid to leave our comfort
zones, and (b) by holding back from doing good to others when
it's in our power to do so.

As wives and mothers, we serve all the time. Serving and
sacrificing for the people we love is part of life, but their
annoying habits and perturbing behaviors can make it a resent-
ful burden, if we let it. And with acquaintances and strangers,
even more so. That's why it's called a sacrifice.

*But to do good and communicate* [to share, associate, to
participate in social intercourse] *forget not: for with such*
*sacrifices God is well pleased. (Hebrews 13:16)*

God promises that when we offer ourselves, when we
sacrifice our time, money, and self for another, He will "open
you the windows of heaven, and pour you out a blessing, that
there shall not be room enough to receive it" (Malachi 3:10).

The Israelites called service to God a weariness (Malachi 1:13). But Galatians 6:9 tells us not to be weary in well doing: for in due season we shall reap, if we faint not. The Israelites balked at presenting God with unblemished flocks, but Romans 12:1 tells us to present our bodies as a holy sacrifice. We can't offer ourselves half-heartedly and expect God to be pleased. We can't withhold what is in our power to give and expect God not to know (Malachi 1:14). The people in Malachi's day lived as they pleased and then came together to "honor" God; it smelled of hypocrisy. "I hate, I despise your feast days, and I will not smell in your solemn assemblies" (Amos 5:21). God regarded their solemn feasts as dung from the animals they sacrificed that He would smear upon their faces—quite a stark metaphor—to make them see how offensive their actions were to Him (Malachi 2:3).

God, through the ministries of His prophets, always warned people before punishing them. Listen and do the right thing, or I will curse your blessings, God spoke in Malachi 2 verse 1. It was out of love for His children that God said this. Why would He bless anyone who disobeyed Him? Doing so would only encourage them to continue living as they pleased. God, throughout His Word, encourages us to turn from our stubbornness and come back to Him. "Return unto me, and I will return unto you," He says in Malachi 3 verse 7. But God has no pleasure in rote oblations. Doing something in the name of God without true, godly love behind it means nothing as Paul eloquently spoke in 1 Corinthians chapter 13.

*Though I speak with the tongues of men and of angels, and have not charity, I am become as sounding brass, or a tinkling cymbal. (1 Corinthians 13:1)*

*And though I have the gift of prophecy, and understand*
*all mysteries, and all knowledge; and though I have all*
*faith, so that I could remove mountains, and have not*
*charity, I am nothing. (1 Corinthians 13:2)*

Because of God's immense love for us, He corrects us as He
did the Israelites of old. Because the character of God does not
change—His love, mercy, goodness, and justice exists forever—
we have hope as they did (Malachi 3:6).

When we seek after God's truth and share that knowledge
with others, we become God's messengers (Malachi 2:7), like
Malachi, whose name means "messenger."[1] When we speak the
truth in love and live by example, admonishing others to turn
away from sin, we are like priests of God (Malachi 2:6). But the
priests recorded in the book of Malachi, not unlike some popular
preachers today, caused many of their flock to stumble or
question the character of God. They corrupted the covenant by
being partial in the law, observing or teaching only parts of the
law and leaving the rest.

*Ye have wearied the Lord with your words. Yet ye say,*
*Wherein have we wearied him? When ye say, Every one*
*that doeth evil is good in the sight of the Lord, and he*
*delighteth in them; or, Where is the God of judgment.*
*(Malachi 2:17)*

The people complained that serving God was in vain
(Malachi 3:14–15). "What profit do we get out of it?" they said.
In their rebellion, they called the proud happy, exalted the
wicked, and the priests did not admonish those who tempted

or mocked God, but by their silence, endorsed their actions. "Woe unto them that call evil good, and good evil; that put darkness for light, and light for darkness; that put bitter for sweet, and sweet for bitter!" (Isaiah 5:20). Calling evil good and good evil is the norm today. People are encouraged to change their genders, abort their babies, steal and destroy property in the name of social justice, hurt others and hate them in the name of entitlement and victimhood. Within the church people defend feminism, homosexuality, and a myriad of other God-opposing issues partial to their own desires and think God approves. "But evil men and seducers shall wax worse and worse, deceiving, and being deceived" (2 Timothy 3:13). Deception is at its worse when people think it doesn't matter how they live after becoming a Christian.

> *Be not deceived; God is not mocked: for whatsoever a man soweth, that shall he also reap.*
> *For he that soweth to his flesh shall of the flesh reap corruption; but he that soweth to the Spirit shall of the Spirit reap life everlasting. (Galatians 6:7–8)*

We know God is faithful and true and will one day completely destroy all evil, but watching the insanity around us, watching evil people prosper and get away with it every day is not only discouraging, but depressing. Even King David lamented, "Behold, these are the ungodly, who prosper in the world; they increase in riches. Verily I have cleansed my heart in vain, and washed my hands in innocency" (Psalm 73:12). But in Malachi 3:5, God promises us He'll be swift to judge sorcery and adultery, swift to judge those who live by lies, swift to judge those who defraud one another, oppress the stranger, the widow, and the fatherless, and swift to judge those who don't fear Him. "For yet a little while," says Psalm 37:10, "and the wicked shall not be: yea, thou shalt diligently consider his place, and it shall not be." Satan, the devourer and originator of every evil and all the pain we've ever felt, will be wholly removed for our sakes (Malachi 3:11).

## The two shall become one

In Malachi, God speaks bluntly of His hatred of divorce, what the King James Version calls "putting away."[2]

*For the Lord, the God of Israel, saith that he hateth putting away: for one covereth violence with his garment, saith the Lord of hosts: therefore take heed to your spirit, that ye deal not treacherously. (Malachi 2:16)*

They Israelites ripped their marriages like one rips off clothes and tried to cover this violence with another garment. Divorce is a violent rending of covenant with your spouse even if you part amicably. The whole of Israel was unfaithful to God by forsaking their true love for Him and marrying another (Malachi 2:11). They were espoused to one Husband but chose strange gods to take His rightful place in their hearts and minds. Not only had they dealt treacherously with God, but they did so with each other. They did not hold their vows sacred. God saw how each man treated his neighbor (Malachi 2:10), and more importantly, how each man treated the wife of his youth (Malachi 2:14), and because of their hypocrisy and unfaithfulness, He refused to listen to their prayers or look upon their offerings.

God made marriage a royal robe without seams, not meant to be torn, so the children that came forth from these unions would be holy to Him (Malachi 2:15). In marriage, two people, a husband and a wife, become one. The goal of marriage is oneness that mirrors the relationship between God, the Father, and His Son, Jesus Christ, and likewise between Christ, the Bridegroom, and His bride, the church (Ephesians 5:31–32).

*Therefore shall a man leave his father and his mother, and shall cleave unto his wife: and they shall be one flesh. (Genesis 2:24)*

*Wherefore they are no more twain, but one flesh. What therefore God hath joined together, let not man put asunder. (Matthew 19:6)*

As a perfect example of oneness throughout the Gospels, Jesus Christ held no separate agenda apart from the Father's. He didn't live for Himself. Christ showed us how to love and gave Himself for the good of mankind. He showed us what a godly, sacrificial marriage should look like by staying true to the Father and putting the Father's will ahead of His own. A marriage cannot prosper if a husband and wife live for themselves. Ideally, husbands guide, nurture, provide for, and protect their wives and families, the same sacrificial service that Christ bestows to His bride. Ideally, wives support their husbands with faithfulness and a willingness to follow their husbands' agendas, giving of themselves for the good of their husbands and families, the same sacrificial service Christ offered to the Father. Many wives in today's culture think they have a right to pursue separate goals outside their husbands' wishes, but that's not what marriage is, and by doing so, the two shall never be one. As Christ's faithful church, our allegiance is to Christ; we don't live for ourselves. As the Father and Son are one (John 10:30), and as Christ and the church are one (Ephesians 5:32), nothing and no one should intrude upon the union of husband and wife.

## John the Baptist

For over 400 years, from the prophet Malachi to John the Baptist, there was no known prophet on the earth.[3] The prophecy concerning John the Baptist is found in two places in the Old Testament: Isaiah 40:3 and Malachi 3:1. Christ, who quoted Malachi, called John the greatest man who ever lived.

> *Verily I say unto you, Among them that are born of women there hath not risen a greater than John the Baptist: notwithstanding he that is least in the kingdom of heaven is greater than he. (Matthew 11:11)*

John was humble. He didn't take on any title or assume any greatness. When the Pharisees asked who he was, he refused to lift himself up. "Art thou Elias? And he saith, I am not. Art thou that prophet? And he answered, No" (John 1:21). Instead, he told them he was the voice crying in the wilderness (Isaiah 40:3). John the Baptist preached the baptism of repentance to prepare people for the kingdom of God (Mark 1:4). He was honored to be the man who baptized Christ Himself, and he was a witness to the heavens parting and the Spirit of God alighting upon Him. John cried in the wilderness, standing outside the comfort and security found in towns, outside the status quo, speaking truth. Would anyone venture outside their comfort zone to hear him? He set the stage for people's hearts to turn toward God, to prepare people for Christ. Many did turn and confess their sins. Centuries before John was born, Malachi 4:5–6 referred to him as Elijah the prophet. Elijah was a mighty and faithful servant of God as John would be.[4]

*And he shall go before him in the spirit and power of Elias* [Elijah]*, to turn the hearts of the fathers to the children, and the disobedient to the wisdom of the just; to make ready a people prepared for the Lord. (Luke 1:17)*

What if your name told the world, as John the Baptist's did, what your main mission or calling from God was? If you were known as Lisa the Uplifter, Amber the Encourager, Janet the Teacher, Cynthia the Server, or Kathy the Comforter, would you more readily live each day using your specific gift to bless your brothers and sisters in Christ and prepare them for the kingdom? John the Baptist prepared hearts to turn toward the Lord. He had a calling and so do we.

*Then they that feared the Lord spake often one to another: and the Lord hearkened, and heard it, and a book of remembrance was written before him for them that feared the Lord, and that thought upon his name. (Malachi 3:16)*

The last chapter of Malachi proclaims a wondrous truth: our names are written in God's book. This is the same book where our tears are stored (Psalm 56:8). Fat tears that shrink our world till all we see is our sorrow through the blur to the scant ones that escape at the kitchen sink, pricking us like a paper cut we least expect. Even if no one else watches them fall, it is comforting to know none of them escape God's notice.

Malachi 3:16 refers to us as "they that feared the Lord." But what does fearing the Lord look like? Fear of the Lord is not merely reverential awe of God's power and righteousness, but recognizing we are morally corrupt, and without Christ in us, we would remain unholy and eternally separated from God. Talk about fear! The fear of the Lord is recognizing that God, through His righteous judgment, has the power to destroy the soul He created if that soul refuses His love. It is knowing that without God, there would be nothing: No love, no joy, no beauty, no world, no body, no thought. Fear of the Lord gives glory to God for the gift of creation, the gift of salvation, and the breathtaking gift of eternal life with Him.

Another standout observation from Malachi 3:16 is that the Lord hears us when we speak to one another or merely think about Him. But many women believe in God or think on His name. Some actually make a living speaking and writing glowing praise about God and how He makes them feel—great swelling words (2 Peter 2:18)—but they don't fear or obey Him, and God will say, "Go away, I never knew you."[5] Believing is not the only criteria for salvation. Even the devils believe in God and tremble (James 2:19). No, the names written in this book of remembrance are those who fear, listen, and obey (in all their imperfect ways), trusting in the God of their salvation to cover them with the righteousness of Christ.

God's original covenant with Levi, the tribe He designated to be priests, was a covenant of life and peace because *they feared*

*Him* (Malachi 2:5). God's covenant with us is the same. And when we uplift and encourage a friend with a verse or two, when we share our stories of how He intervened and saved us, when we pray throughout the day and thank Him for the bird sitting on the wall or the brilliant sunset or the sale at the store we weren't expecting, the baby's first steps, and the teens getting along—He hears it all. How thrilling it is, and quite sobering, to know God has collected all the names of His faithful and inscribed them with holy ink.

> *And they shall be mine, saith the Lord of hosts, in that day*
> *when I make up my jewels; and I will spare them, as a*
> *man spareth his own son that serveth him. (Malachi 3:17)*

And because we think on His name out of love and reverence, God will set us as jewels. As flawless gems, we will gleam in the palm of His hand. God will spare us His wrath because in that day we will reflect the glory of His Son. "In that day" is not only the day of destruction for the wicked but the day of luminous transformation for all of us who love God and have waited patiently for Him (1 Corinthians 15:51–52).

> *But unto you that fear my name shall the Sun of*
> *righteousness arise with healing in his wings; and ye shall*
> *go forth, and grow up as calves of the stall. (Malachi 4:2)*

Christ, the Sun of righteousness, the day star, the bright and morning star,[6] whose love is like a warm embrace, will permanently heal us from the blemishes, scars, and deformities that sin has spawned in us. Christ, the Son of righteousness, ushers in a new age. A new day will dawn, but this dawn is permanent; it becomes new and stays new. "Behold, I make all things new" (2 Corinthians 5:17; Revelation 21:5).

The book of Malachi, like each of the books of the Minor Prophets, warns and challenges and offers us hope with a grand glimpse of the brilliance of Christ's righteous light that awaits us in His coming kingdom.

> For the Lord God is a sun and shield: the Lord will give grace and glory: no good thing will he withhold from them that walk uprightly. (Psalm 84:11)

As we look forward to that day, struggling in a world bent on wickedness, let us women of God continue to apply our curious minds and faithful hearts unto His wisdom.

Speak, my friends, of God with fear.
Speak often one to another. He hears!
Declare His goodness,
Proclaim His mercy,
Bid others gaze with you His mighty works.
And teach, teach with love, His Word of truth.

# What's the story behind...?

*But who may abide the day of his coming? and who shall stand when he appeareth? for he is like a refiner's fire, and like **fullers' soap**. (Malachi 3:2)*

Fire was (and still is) used to purify precious metals, but who or what are fullers? Fulling is a process for cleansing and whitening shorn wool to eliminate oils, dirt, and other impurities. Fullers would beat the newly-woven cloth soaked in alkali soap to brighten it and cause the opposing fibers to interlock, forming a more sturdy and useful textile.[7]

Our Christian growth process often feels like being pummeled and stretched and forced into uncomfortable positions. But the outcome produces a clean and resilient faith. We will be completely cleansed of all unrighteousness at Christ's return, leaving only the purity of Christ in us to shine.

# Malachi notes

1. *Strong's* reference H4401, taken from H4397.
2. *Strong's* reference H7971. See also H3748: a *cutting* (of the matrimonial bond), *divorce*; and G647.
3. "What Happened Between the Old and New Testament?," *Olive Tree Blog*, accessed on April 25, 2025, https://www.olivetree.com/blog/what-happened-between-old-and-new-testament/.
4. See 1 Kings 17–19 and 2 Kings 1–2.
5. See Matthew 7:21–23 and Luke 13:25–27.
6. See 2 Peter 1:19 and Revelation 22:16.
7. "Fuller," *Smith's Bible Dictionary*, Bible Study Tools, accessed on April 25, 2025, https://www.biblestudytools.com/dictionary/fuller/.

# Appendix

For those who are curious, I've compiled a brief list of definitions and summaries for the three differing views on eschatology, which is the branch of theology concerned with the final events (end times) of human history.

**Amillennialism:** the denial that an earthly millennium of universal righteousness and peace will either precede or follow the second advent of Jesus Christ.[1]

Amillennialists do not believe in a literal one-thousand-year event, but believe the millennium is happening right now in heaven with believers resurrected at death.[2]

**Postmillennialism:** the theological doctrine that the second coming of Christ will occur after the millennium.[3]

Postmillennialists also do not believe in a one-thousand-year timeframe. They believe this world will continue to get better or "Christianized," and afterward Christ will return.[4]

**Premillennialism**: the view that Christ's return will usher in a future millennium of Messianic rule mentioned in Revelation.[5]

Premillennialism is split into two subsections or systems, (a) dispensational premillennialism, and (b) historic premillennialism. There are a few sub-sub views within premillennialism not listed here.

- **Dispensational premillennialist** believe in seven "dispensations" or ages in history, and they believe that Israel and the church are distinct entities.[6] In their view (popularized in 1830), Jesus Christ will rapture Christians to heaven immediately *before the seven-year tribulation* and bring them with Him at His second coming. They believe in a future restoration of the nation of Israel, and believe physical Israel will live and reign on earth during the millennium.

- **Historic premillennialists** believe the church, this present age of grace, was predicted in the Old Testament prophecies.[7] Historic premillenialists believe Christ will rapture the church *after the tribulation*. They believe that God's promises concerning the nation of Israel are fulfilled by the church, and Israel will not have a separate role in Christ's millennial kingdom apart from the church.

# Appendix notes

1. Merriam-Webster online dictionary, s.v. "Amillennialism," accessed April 25, 2025, https://www.merriam-webster.com/dictionary/amillennialism.

2. "What is amillennialim?," GotQuestions.org, accessed April 25, 2025, https://www.gotquestions.org/amillennialism.html.

3. Merriam-Webster online dictionary, s.v. "Postmillennialism," accessed April 25, 2025, https://www.merriam-webster.com/dictionary/postmillennialism.

4. "What is postmillennialism?," GotQuestions.org, accessed April 25, 2025, https://www.gotquestions.org/postmillennialism.html.

5. Merriam-Webster online dictionary, s.v. "Premillennialism," accessed April 25, 2025, https://www.merriam-webster.com/dictionary/premillennialism.

6. Timothy J, Demy and Thomas Ice, "What is Premillennialism?," Crosswalk.com, April 26, 2022, accessed April 25, 2025, https://www.crosswalk.com/faith/bible-study/what-is-premillenialism.html.

7. "Historic premillennialism—What is it?," CompellingTruth.org, accessed April 25, 2025, https://www.compellingtruth.org/historic-premillennialism.html.

# About the Author

Gleniece Lytle is a writer, editor, and Bible study enthusiast. As a curious woman, she wondered what the unusual words she found in her King James Version Bible meant, which lead her to research and write a popular series for her blog, Desert Rain. Gleniece also writes a monthly newsletter, *Abide & Blossom*, to uplift the weary Christian women living in the chaos of our times. When not writing, she serves nonfiction authors with her editing and typesetting business, Desert Rain Editing. Faith and obedience to Christ has turned her once parched life into a well-watered garden.

Gleniece lives in Arizona in an unfinished desert cabin with Douglas, her husband of over forty years. She home-schooled all five of her children and loved to learn something new every day along with them. Contemplating the goodness of God always leaves her awe-struck, like gazing at the rich turquoise, magenta, and tangerine palette of a desert sunset.

She's happiest with a glass of red wine, a piece of dark chocolate, and is positively giddy when a graceful pirouette of words that perfectly captures what she'd been struggling with for days leaps onto the page and bows.

You can connect with Gleniece at desertraingleniece.com, sign up for her monthly newsletter, *Abide & Blossom*, and visit desertrainediting.com for your editing and typesetting needs.

www.ingramcontent.com/pod-product-compliance
Lightning Source LLC
Chambersburg PA
CBHW061749120626
46550CB00005B/1938